FINDI[illegible]IT
M[illegible]GE

HOW TO TURN VOICE OF CUSTOMER RESEARCH
INTO IRRESISTIBLE WEBSITE COPY

JENNIFER HAVICE

MM

PRAISE FOR FINDING THE RIGHT MESSAGE

"If you want to get into customers' heads and move them to action, this is THE book you need to make sense of the 'how.' The practices Jen gives away here are the secret weapons behind the results of copywriters to multimillion (or multibillion) dollar brands. I know, because I use them every single time I write.

Best of all, Jen has found a way to make these lessons accessible to anyone, not just the pros.

So grab a pen: you're going to want to take notes."

Joel Klettke
Founder of Business Casual Copywriting and Case Study Buddy

"Just when I think I've hit the ceiling of insight I can pull out of voice-of-the-customer research, Jen Havice pipes up and shows me a whole new level of value I can bring to the table for my clients. Run, don't walk, to order the updated edition of this awesome book."

Jessica Mehring
CEO of Horizon Peak Consulting

“Not only is Jen Havice’s excellent book the absolute last word on how to *find* the right message, but – particularly in this new, updated edition – it’s also the most reliable and comprehensive resource on how to *use* the right message once you’ve found it (oftentimes an even more useful thing to know).

I can’t count how many times I’ve recommended (or even insisted) that a colleague, friend, client, or prospect stop what they’re doing with their marketing and not start again until they’ve read this book.

With the second edition’s updated tool lists, deeper dive into Jobs To Be Done theory, and expanded explanations on how to use the messages you find, I can already see that I’ll be recommending and insisting people read it for the next 4 years (and more) as well.”

James E. Turner
Conversion Copywriter & Owner of
TurnerCreative + SNAP Copy

“Jen’s book opened my eyes to the concepts, process, and application of customer research, all of which help me to get the best possible results for my clients. It’s the only hard copy book that I carry with me while I work and travel, because it is literally worth its weight!"

Rachael Pilcher
Founder of Mighty Fine Copy

"Be honest, you KNOW you should be doing more customer research. How else are you going to get the insights you need to instantly convince your ideal customers both that you truly understand their struggles, *and* that you're uniquely qualified to erase them? But I get it – customer research is A Lot. Where the heck do you start?! Jen Havice's ***Finding The Right Message*** is where. This shining gem of a book is a concise, jargon-free and wholly practical guide for anyone who wants to stop guessing at their messaging – and sell more stuff. If your copy of the first edition is anything like as well-loved as mine, you're going to love the fresh ideas (and spanking new cover) of this revised edition. If you're brand new to Havice's genius – welcome! You're in for a rare (and deeply actionable) treat!"

Gin Walker
Founder of Gin Walker Words

“As a content marketer and copywriter, I've learned the hard way that not investing upfront in nailing down the right message will catch up with you later. Finding The Right Message provides a simple approach to discovering the right message for your audience and is packed full of actionable insights for every marketer and copywriter. This book is a must-read if you care about the customer journey and making more sales, and I recommend it to anyone who will listen”

Maggie Patterson
Editorial Director, Scoop Studios

“Jen's practical advice in this book is a must-read — even (maybe especially) if you're a marketer who thinks you “know” your customers inside and out. From explaining why customer research is so important and outlining common organizational barriers against conducting meaningful research, to explaining six elements of effective messaging, to guidance on survey creation and instructions for analyzing customer reviews, this book offers everything you need to know to start asking the right questions at the right time.”

Lianna Patch
Founder of Punchline Conversion Copywriting

FINDING THE RIGHT MESSAGE
How to Turn Voice of Customer Research Into Irresistible Website Copy

Second Edition
By Jennifer Havice

Make Mention Media and Communications LLC

Internet websites listed in this work may have changed or disappeared between when this work was written and when it is read.

ISBN: 978-0-578-64871-2 (ebook)

ISBN: 978-0-578-64872-9 (paperback)

Cover Design by: Jessica Reed

www.makementionmedia.com

PREFACE TO THE SECOND EDITION

I published the first edition in 2016. While the term "conversion copywriter" wasn't brand spanking new at the time, customer research as part and parcel of the copywriter's job to drive conversions across the digital funnel hadn't exactly taken hold either. Sure, the good copywriters were doing research and measuring results in one form or another, but those who truly understood how to listen to their customers and integrate their findings into cohesive messaging strategies and copywriting were few and far between.

This situation has changed. More and more copywriters and marketers have learned not only the importance of voice of customer research but what to do with it to create and optimize their copy.

Except, the questions remain about conducting and applying voice of customer research - particularly with the explosion of online marketing tools. Which are the best tools to use for surveys? Should I be relying on heat maps? Is there an easier way to categorize my survey results? The list goes on.

I also continue to get asked about the role of personas in messaging and when to show prospects and customers the right messages throughout the customer journey.

I understand the confusion. It's a big part of the reason I wrote the book in the first place: to give small business owners, in particular, a guide to navigating how to more thoughtfully and effectively communicate with their website visitors.

While entrepreneurs and small business owners have embraced and used the ideas in this book, copywriters and marketers have broadened their reach. They're the people landing in my inbox, asking the questions, and discussing the ins and outs of getting the most from their customer research.

This second edition reflects the needs of and conversations with this expanded target audience and a subtle shift in how I tackle messaging research for my clients. Here are the fundamental changes in this edition:

- Part One is now devoted to understanding the concept of your customer's "why" and the six elements of effective messaging that underpin every voice of customer research project I do. I'll delve more deeply into Jobs To Be Done Theory and its impact on my approach to conducting and assessing voice of customer research.

- Parts Two, Three, and Four focus on the "how-to" behind gathering and utilizing your customer research. I go into more detail about categorizing and compiling your survey responses. I've updated any resources and tools that may be the most helpful as you embark on your research and writing journey. You'll find the names along with thoughts on when to reach for a tool, including options depending on your needs.

If you've read the First Edition and found it useful, I'm confident you'll discover new insights to apply to your research and copywriting. If you're picking up *Finding The Right Message* for the first time, welcome to the world of listening to your customers.

INTRODUCTION

It's time for a reality check. When was the last time you thought about why your customers come to your website? If you can't remember, don't feel bad. You're not alone. Most people focus on what they find most valuable when they are putting together their website. Today that ends.

Instead of thinking about your copy as just words on the page, words that communicate information, I want you to start thinking about it as the key to helping your customers achieve their goals. Because your copy—make that, your entire website—has less to do with you than you might think. It's about what your visitors need to get from Point A to Point Z, and everywhere in between.

You're probably thinking, "*Yeah, but what about my business goals? How can I make those happen if I'm just thinking about what my customers want?*"

Therein lies the secret. Your goals are tied to those of your customers.

The question you need to ask yourself is, "How do I help my customers achieve their goals on my website while still achieving my own?"

Let's just say that your customers think their motivations, hesitations, and fears have everything to do with how you frame your copy and the words you use. Giving your website visitors the information they need at the right time, and using the words that most resonate with them, makes it far easier for them to decide to buy into what you're selling.

And if your potential customers can easily make that decision, your conversions and revenues will go through the roof.

That is if you start listening to those people.

When you ask the right questions, you get answers that help you develop high performing copy that practically writes itself

If you've ever tried writing a sales page or even an email when you have no idea who your best-fit customers are, you'll know how difficult it is. As one of my clients recently told me, "It feels like throwing words up against a wall and waiting to see what sticks." When you don't know who is most likely to purchase from you and why you'll be struggling to give them reasons to choose you over the competition, you'll have a tough time helping those same people understand how much value they'll get from the features they care most about or why their biggest hesitations to purchase aren't that big of a deal.

Want to get more of the people who will become long-term, high-value customers to open your emails, move from free-trial to paid, or jump at the chance to buy your newest offering?

Customer research is the critical piece of the puzzle that makes every launch, blog post, or product description resonate and connect with those who matter most to your business.

But, customer research is still the kale nobody wants to put in their marketing or product development smoothie

As someone who spends her time obsessing about messaging strategy and customer-driven copywriting for clients, I'd love to say companies dedicated to learning what makes their customers tick is the norm these days. Sadly, it's not. And there are cold, hard, sad numbers to prove it.

ProfitWell, a provider of analytics software for subscription businesses, reached out to SaaS and subscription executives and product leaders to see if companies were doing more than merely extolling the virtues of customer research.

Here is what they found:

- 7 out of 10 companies speak to less than ten prospects or customers a month in a non-sales, research capacity.
- Almost half of these companies conduct ZERO tests a month (including marketing.)
- Out of the last 5k features built, product leaders said the vast majority were differentiable and highly valuable while the 1.2 million customers surveyed indicated most were not.

The problems don't end with building products and features customers consider marginally valuable. According to Salesforce's 2019 State of the Connected Customer report, 84% of customers say the company's experience is as relevant as its products and services.

And, that's up from 80% the year before.

With the exponential growth of content online, potential customers have become better educated and savvier. They can do their research, stake out the competition, and jump ship as soon as their expectations haven't been met. Consistently and continuously learning as much as possible about your customers is more critical than ever.

Customer research has more than a PR problem

After working with B2B and B2C clients over the years, I've noticed a few key reasons businesses are talking but not walking the walk.

No leadership buy-in

Conducting research takes time, costs money, and can be challenging to tie to an immediate ROI. Unless leaders in the organization have bought into the need and long-term payoff of investing in understanding their customers, customer research will always be a tough sell.

Lack of internal resources

Not every company can keep someone on staff solely responsible for conducting interviews, designing surveys, or running user testing sessions. Without someone accountable, customer research can quickly take a back seat to just about anything else that seems more pressing or remotely more attractive (*unless you love geeking out over data and spreadsheets.*)

Siloed thinking

Sales, marketing, customer success, every department has its priorities, ideas, and ways of doing things. Like anything in life, cross-department cooperation isn't a problem until **it's a problem.** For instance, when you're trying to coordinate your messaging, streamline your onboarding process or get the most out of your customer research, you need to make sure your teams are all on the same page. Nothing kills the joy of discovering breathtaking new insights about your customers faster than team members who don't agree with the process, findings, or changes to be made.

An expertise gap

Even if you've got a marketing or sales team member who digs running A/B tests or discovering where the hiccups are in generating new leads, they need to know what questions to ask, what data to look at, and how to synthesize the information in a way that can be accessible to everyone. Frequently, having someone on the team whose enthusiasm matches the necessary skill set can be a rare commodity.

Inertia

Listening to your customers takes time, commitment, and patience. Not surprisingly, customer research tends to be the first item on the agenda to go and the last to be added back on when fires need to be put out, or deadlines loom. Like any other aspect of growing a business that can be labor-intensive and have a long runway to benefits (think content marketing), it's way easier to pay lip service to customer research than actually doing it. And it can be tricky to know where to start. Because you need to have a clear idea of your goals and which categories and types of research will help you get the job done.

Quantitative and qualitative... yes, you should be doing both even if you don't want to

Quantitative research tells us what's happening and where. It includes analytics, behavior tracking, and A/B testing on your websites, apps, and email campaigns. Whether you're seeking to improve conversions on your website or reduce customer acquisition costs, you need to know your baseline and where the stumbling blocks are.

If quantitative research informs the "what," qualitative research helps us understand the "why." Open-ended customer surveys, interviews, user testing, are all tools in the qualitative toolbox. When implemented well, they can get straight to the heart of your customers' motivations, desired outcomes, hesitations to purchase, and so much more.

As the Profitwell numbers and my own experience working with businesses mentioned earlier suggest, making a well-rounded customer research strategy happen can be a challenge. You may be able to figure out where the bottlenecks are in the customer journey, but tying those to why prospects bounce off your checkout page or churn in droves three months into a subscription involves more than mere numbers. You need to talk to those best-fit customers to understand what messages and experiences will move them from prospect to customer to raving fan.

Here's a little secret: none of that matters unless you have a strategy for turning all of those insights into copywriting that connects the dots between the job your solution has to get done in the eyes of your customers and the ongoing value it provides. For a lot of people, connecting those dots can be the most daunting task of all.

Why I decided to write this book in the first place

Type the word "copywriting" in Amazon's search bar, and you'll find over 3,000 results. From Sugarman to Bly and Edwards to everyone in between, you can get your hands on copywriting and messaging advice from the world's most successful marketers. Admittedly, adding another book to the mix won't tell us anything we don't already know, right? That's what I thought until I started piecing everything I had learned about optimizing existing copy and developing persuasive messaging in a step-by-step process based on customer research. Every time I searched for a concise go-to resource about doing the research and then applying it to my copy, I left with more questions than answers.

I knew if I struggled early on, others had to have too. After years of working with clients on my own and collaborating with others in the industry, I decided to share what I had learned.

This book will be your guide to conducting customer research and then putting your findings to good use when writing your website copy or coming up with an overall messaging strategy. You'll get a straightforward methodology for getting the right data, glean the most important takeaways, and use your findings to create copywriting that boosts your bottom line.

Who is this book intended for?

This book is for anyone who wants to stop guessing which messages will turn prospects into customers online but is unsure where to start. This list includes:

- In-house or freelance marketers who need to generate more leads and convert more visitors into customers
- Copywriters who need to create a persuasive, compelling piece of copy at each stage of the customer journey
- Business owners who need to understand better what differentiates their offerings in the marketplace and how to talk about them in ways that keep their customers coming back for more

Don't worry if you're new to qualitative research. I've kept the book as straightforward, jargon-free, and actionable as possible. There are no complex matrices or unintelligible frameworks to decipher. Nor is this book meant to be a comprehensive textbook on customer research, filled with talk of reaching statistical significance. Instead, think of this book as a guide to get you started on the road to finding out about your ideal customers. My goal is to help you communicate more effectively with the people coming to your website who are most likely to buy so that you can sell more.

How best to use this book

This book is split into four parts:

- Part 1: Understanding Your Customer's Why
- Part 2: Getting Your Voice of Customer Research
- Part 3: Analyzing the Research
- Part 4: Applying What You've Learned to Your Website Copy

I suggest you read through the entire book once to get a clear understanding of how the whole process works from start to finish. Then go through it again to gather your research.

Finally, plan to experiment and test. Some questions and messages work better than others. While I provide you with examples and scripts, remember that *your* business, website, and visitors are unique. Try different things and learn from the results. If one survey question doesn't bring in the number of responses you need, tweak your question and move onto round two. Keep testing, continue learning, and never stop talking to your customers.

PART I

UNDERSTANDING YOUR CUSTOMER'S WHY

1

REFRAME HOW YOU THINK ABOUT THE MESSAGES YOU SERVE TO YOUR CUSTOMERS

When was the last time you landed on a product's website or clicked through an ad to a landing page and got sucked into reading?

The messages resonated. The copy seemed laser targeted to overcoming a particular problem. It didn't take a Ph.D. to figure out how the solution would make your life a lot better.

If you can't remember, don't feel bad.

Most marketing copy falls short. Jargon-riddled, feature-laden, and lifeless. It's copywriting and messaging that focuses far more on how the product performs than the value it provides - leaving prospective customers wondering why they should care enough to keep reading or take the next step towards purchasing.

That's a problem, a huge problem.

You've only got a few seconds to draw someone in once they land on your site. Based on a study by Microsoft, the folks over at the Nielsen Norman Group say that you have all of ten seconds to clearly articulate your value proposition to keep people engaged longer. There's a high likelihood that people will click away without a compelling reason to stay within those first few seconds.

Call it dwindling attention spans, information overload, impatience, or simply laziness; the reality is that people don't want to think when they first land on a web page. They want to immediately know if they're going to find what they're looking for on your site.

Which brings me back to the importance of knowing not only what your customers expect when they land on your website but also the kinds of words they use when they think about your product and what sort of challenge they hope to overcome with your product's help.

Let's do a little exercise. Imagine trying to decide between grabbing a meal at two different burger joints operating side by side with only thirty seconds to make a decision. To make things more interesting, you're a vegetarian. Eating organic is important to you, as well as steering clear of processed foods.

You quickly glance at the menus for both restaurants and find a veggie burger option on each one. *Phew!* You think to yourself. *At least I'll have something to eat.* With a few seconds left to make your decision, you notice a sign above the menu on one of the restaurant's windows that says, "We only use organic ingredients harvested from sustainable farms and ranches."

The words *organic, harvested,* and *sustainable* leap out at you. They are words you actively seek out when shopping at the grocery store. As if by magic, they have appeared in precisely the right spot at the right time to catch your attention. Decision made. You walk into the restaurant without so much as a second thought.

It may seem like a silly hypothetical situation (and not just the vegetarian part if you're a lifelong meat-eater), but this is what happens every minute of every day online. Posed with multiple websites selling similar products and services, most of us will keep hitting the back button and resuming our search for what we want until a compelling message gives us a reason to stop looking.

Consider this: Those same researchers at the Nielsen Norman Group found that 79 percent of their test users scanned any new page they came across, with only 16 percent reading word by word. With limited time and cognitive resources, people will settle for "good enough" when looking for answers that meet their essential needs. Psychologists call this "satisficing," a combination of the words *satisfy* and *suffice.*

As in the restaurant example, website visitors latch onto the chunks of information that make it easiest for them to reach a decision. Your task is to figure out which words and phrases will get your visitors to stop dead in their tracks and move them to take the desired action that fits their needs, goals, and expectations. To do that, you need to find out who your ideal customers are and what makes them tick.

Too many businesses rely on irrelevant information or no information when understanding their customers

Personas, avatars, whatever you want to call them, product developers, and marketers have been using these fictional representations of buyers to decide what to sell and how to sell for years. Based on customer research data, buyer personas are tools designed to help businesses understand who makes up their target audiences and what influences their buying choices.

At least they should be. The problem with most personas is that they have been put together with either irrelevant data or no data at all. Many personas are built around a profile of what the business would like its ideal buyer to be instead of representing the buyer's expectations, needs, wants, and concerns. In other words, we're talking about wishful thinking, not necessarily reality.

A messaging disconnect

A few years ago, I began helping a local nonprofit organization market its resale shop online. I remember my first visit to the shop. Nice and tidy, it had all the trappings of a small retail store selling clothing and housewares. Volunteer sales associates bustled around, helping customers, and displaying newly received items.

My first impression was of a homier, warmer version of Goodwill. All the donated items on sale looked to be in excellent condition. Most folks' shopping appeared to be people from the community that the larger parent organization helped support. So I was a bit startled when I found out who the marketing team identified as their ideal customer. The persona they described amounted to a woman in her fifties living in the highest rent district in town with discriminating tastes that leaned far closer to Tiffany's than Target.

"Is this who shops in the store?" I asked.

"Not really. Except we do have quite a few volunteers who buy things," one of them said.

After more questions and multiple marketing meetings, I started to realize there was a profound disconnect between who the team wanted to market to and who their actual customers were. The core group of volunteers who spearheaded the creation of the shop had a vision of a high-end resale boutique. They would concentrate on taking in designer donations and cultivate a clientele with disposable assets.

The reality was quite different. The shop didn't look and feel like a high-end boutique, nor did it attract the type of customers the marketing team aspired to bring in, which meant the messaging they dished out consistently fell on deaf ears.

Don't get caught in the buyer persona trap

Unfortunately, the resale shop marketing team's experience is all too common. Many businesses rely on creative thinking in determining their target audiences without learning how or why their customers make buying decisions. They pull out a stock photo of a person who meets the basic demographics of their customers (or who they want their customers to be), slap a name on it, and make assumptions about what drives behavior.

It's easy to fall into this trap. Go online, and you'll find templates, articles, and blog posts littering the web with illustrations of buyer personas similar to these. The problem is that assumption-driven personas fail marketers and businesses in several ways:

- They focus on a Mad Libs approach based on preconceived notions of the customer. These types of personas lean almost exclusively on educated guesswork and your ideas about your customers. This guesswork can lead to biased decision making about what you think is important to your customers instead of what actually moves the needle with your messaging and copy.
- They don't tell you why your customers make decisions. Most personas use demographic data (e.g., gender, age, income) for their customer profiles. Factors like age and gender may help provide a fuller picture of your customers, but those kinds of statistics leave out the why behind the action. Rather than spelling out the crucial things like purchase drivers or hesitations, they encourage the creation of a one-dimensional image of your customers.
- They rarely lead to actionable insights or discernable outcomes. Over the years, clients have shared personas they've created on their own and ones developed by expensive consultants. Each time I ask what kind of impact the persona work has had on their businesses, I find that it has ended up in the equivalent of the virtual junk drawer without a second look. Whether it's the marketing, sales,

or product team, none of them find these personas particularly useful.

Let's think of buyer personas in a slightly different way

So, why are we even talking about buyer personas if most of them are completely useless? As of the writing of this book, 7.3 million results appear in a Google search for the term. Marketers and businesses still consider personas a tool worth pursuing and find it a hot topic to read and write about relentlessly. That's why I feel it's important to explain where personas fit into the process outlined in this book. Think of personas this way: when buyer personas are based on the thoughts, feelings, and stories behind how and why people make purchasing decisions, they are a representation of useful voice of customer research.

Buyer personas built without the guesswork will provide you with a repeatable process to inform your marketing and product development. In essence, it's a similar process to what I'll be showing you how to do here. Except, our focus will be on gaining insights to optimize the copy on your website with relevant data and a slightly different approach to how we look at your product in relation to your customers. You can say goodbye to spending time picking out stock photographs or monikers for your personas. Instead, you'll map out what messages will give you the biggest return on investment by asking the right questions, deftly interpreting the answers, and applying what you've learned with a nifty little framework I've developed.

Your product has a job to do

But before we can dive into the nitty-gritty of finding your messages, we need to talk about one more mindset shift. It's a shift not only in how you understand your customers but also in how they think about your product. It's a shift that has helped shape product development over the last few decades and the way I approach every research and messaging project.

If you've been in marketing or product development for any length of time, you've probably heard of Jobs To Be Done Theory (JTBD.) Harvard professor, Clayton Christensen, and Bob Moesta (among others) developed JTBD to understand customer behavior better and discover how to create products and services customers will *actually* buy.

They noticed more than two decades ago that seemingly successful companies failed despite the volume and variety of information they had about their customers. These companies would try to innovate and stay competitive only to find themselves losing ground.

Their conclusion: these companies weren't asking the right questions to find out what was most important to their customers. Instead of digging deep into the reasons why their customers made the choices they did, these companies focused on making their products better or different from the competition - not necessarily into what their customers needed to help them achieve their goals.

Your customers are "hiring" your product to make progress in a particular circumstance

Jobs To Be Done Theory centers around the idea that products exist to get a job done in a customer's life. For instance, I've been struggling with getting enough fruits and vegetables in the middle of the day while I'm either working or running around, taking care of the business of life. While I'd love to say that I'm juicing a variety of organic fruits and vegetables in between client calls and chasing after my dogs, it's not happening.

But, that bottle of organic, specialty fruit and kale juice I picked up at the market the other day works. It perfectly caters to addressing my moment of struggle - how to eat healthy on the go and without the prep. I'm probably not going to choose a bottle of juice to replace dinners, but in this particular circumstance, it got the job done.

Why viewing your messages through a JTBD lens can transform how you approach your copy

When you're developing an innovative product, people will buy, you have to know all the details of your customers' choices, what keeps them up at night, and makes their heads spin. The same holds for unearthing the critical messages your prospects and customers need to see along with putting together the copy that drives action.

With Jobs To Be Done as a lens, not only can you more easily focus on what to include in your messaging *(and what to leave out)* but also how to do it in a way that improves conversions.

Here's why:

JTBD emphasizes the customer's struggle before the solution.

At its core, JTBD is based on the idea that solutions may come and go, but the struggles people seek to overcome stay the same. What people choose to help them make progress at any given time has more to do with the emotional and social factors going on in their lives than merely the functional aspects (or feature sets) of one solution over another.

In the book, Competing Against Luck: The Story of Innovation and Customer Choice, Clayton Christensen uses the example of childcare to illustrate this point. Trusting who will take care of your child more than likely will be the deciding factor. The where, what, and how come in a distant second. The struggle is always the same. How you solve for it depends on the circumstances in your life and your motivation for doing so. In the case of childcare, you could send your child to daycare, pay for a full-time nanny, get the grandparents to chip in, or do a combination of all three. Each solution may compete or work in tandem with one another.

The key is to understand your customers' struggles within the context of their lives and the job they need your product or solution to get done for them. When you've done that, you're in a much better position to spell out the value your daycare, bottle of kale juice, or widget provides to the people most likely to buy from you.

JTBD focuses on why customers make the choices they do in their own words.

When you approach your messaging investigation from the customer's perspective and the struggle they're trying to overcome; you start to understand how your product fits into their life. Suddenly, it becomes clear what triggering events happen to motivate someone to seek your product out or what's getting in the way of purchasing in the first place. All of this can have profound effects on your copywriting and implications for how you help prospects and customers along on their journey.

Consider the story of Intercom, a company that develops software for real-time messaging between businesses. In 2011, the founder, Des Traynor, decided to take a JTBD approach to learn why people sought the solution out and what problems the solution fixed for them. Using interviews designed to dig deep into what had been happening in their customers' lives leading up to the decision to sign up (anxieties holding them back and pressures were pushing them to solve their problems) he not only discovered that his customers were coming to Intercom to tackle several different jobs but also that his team wasn't even using the same words to describe their solution as their customers. Their customers continually referred to how they used Intercom as a way to "engage" with their customers, not as an "outbound messaging" tool (the term used by Intercom.)

As Des mentioned in a Harvard Business Review interview about the JTBD process, "Essentially, we realized that we'd been offering a one-size-fits-none service. The initial price felt high because no customer needed everything we were selling." With this knowledge, Intercom developed four different service offerings to address the key jobs their customers needed to get done, including helping Intercom's customers observe, engage with, learn from, and support their customers.

The upshot: their conversion rates increased, and they found a "logical path for relationship growth." JTBD served as a catalyst for change in how Intercom approached their business and how they thought about their customers and what they needed to hear to make a buying decision.

If you're thinking, "That's all well and good, but I just want better copywriting. My business is fine. Thank you very much." I get it. You probably didn't pick up this book looking for advice on rethinking your products, services, or business model. Here's the thing: once you start asking your customers questions about their behaviors and teasing apart the causes behind why they make buying decisions, you begin to see your product or solution from an entirely new perspective. Your piece of software, consulting service, or beverage becomes more than merely the sum of its feature set. Its real value derives from how well it can move your customers along the path to achieving their goal (or getting their job done.) Once you've wrapped your head around that, you're better able to find the disconnects within your messaging and offerings that confuse or turn off your website visitors. And, that can be the difference between success and failure of your business online.

How do you leap from theory to practice?

The next step is to put into practice these ideas about your customers in a systematic way that produces highly compelling and converting messages. If you're freaking out because that sounds like a big, scary, mess of a project, don't worry. I'm going to show you exactly how the sausage is made to help you make sense of the process. The best way to start is by walking through the six key elements that define your messaging. That way, you'll be armed with a framework to organize all the incredible insights you gather from your research.

2

SIX ELEMENTS OF EFFECTIVE MESSAGING

When I first started learning the ins and outs of copywriting, customer research, and optimization, I kept arriving at the same question without a clear answer.

What information do I need to get from my prospects and customers to write better-performing copy consistently?

It seemed like a simple enough question. The problem was that when it came to optimizing the copy for websites (or any part of the online funnel for that matter), I had a tough time finding something akin to a straightforward roadmap to follow. It's not enough to have a process for extracting the right information; you need to know what you're searching for and how to organize it reliably. Otherwise, it's too easy to get lost in teasing apart the important from the inconsequential in your messages.

Your customers are taking a journey from struggle to success

You've probably heard the adage, "If you sell to everyone, you sell to no one." When it comes to writing copy that converts visitors into customers, your goal is to tap into those messages visitors need to see before making a decision. Your key to finding those messages specific to your best-fit customers lies in knowing their particular journey from the struggle before using your solution to success after incorporating it into their lives.

The six elements of effective messaging that follow will help you do just that. Built on ideas from persuasive copywriting, Jobs To Be Done Theory, and my years of working in the field, they combine to paint a picture of your customers' lives before, during, and after your solution entered the scene.

Struggle

Whether you're deciding on a place to have dinner or which web hosting service to switch to, you're looking to solve a problem. You're hungry, or your website server sucks. You have an issue you're struggling with and need someone or something to fix it.

The distress experienced without a fix is the pain that leads to an ongoing struggle to be resolved. Successful products and services address their customers' struggles and alleviate them so customers can make progress in their lives. If you have ever tried to sell something that no one seemed the least interested in buying, chances are it didn't solve a real problem, or you weren't marketing it to the right audience.

Let's use a product that's tangible and easy to understand as an example: contemporary handmade jewelry.

You're probably thinking, "*What kind of pain does a necklace solve? It's a necklace, not a cancer drug.*"

A necklace or a pair of earrings can solve a pain point. You simply need to view the situation from your customer's perspective. Let's say you're a high-powered executive woman who needs to look professional in every way while in the office and out with clients, except your tastes run a little edgy. You're no Audrey Hepburn in *Breakfast at Tiffany's with pearls and a twin-set as your default.*

Your jewelry is one place where you feel like you can exercise a bit of freedom. The struggle becomes finding an accessory that allows you to express your chic personality while remaining professional. What's motivating you to do that may be a desire to show more of your authentic self or simply feel more attractive. That desired outcome fuels the need to alleviate the immediate pain and ongoing struggle of dressing for success.

The Fix

In the case of our necklace example, that piece of jewelry gets the job done of helping our fictitious hip executive express her personality without looking like she just walked in from a Grateful Dead concert. The necklace provides a fix for a specific problem this customer has (albeit one that may not seem readily apparent or as a source of pain to everyone.)

Whether you're selling a physical product or a service, the fix comes directly from your target-market customers and the struggle they're trying to overcome. Keep in mind that it may not be the same fix you envisioned before talking to those customers.

I saw this disconnect play out in a project I worked on several years ago. I had been tasked with doing voice of customer research for a company that marketed its software as a content management system loaded with marketing bells and whistles. While the product did help businesses easily set up websites and market themselves more effectively, the people getting the most value from the products framed its job of in different terms. They needed an all-in-one media platform that made it easy to promote and grow their businesses. Sure, this piece of software could do this job, but the best-fit customers had a tough time figuring out the existing website. The copy focused more on an easy way to build a content marketing toolset than a way for profitable authors and podcasters to showcase and market their content.

For this company, the research exposed more than just an issue with their messaging and website copy. They had to contend with gaping holes in their positioning strategy. Not only had they been marketing to a poor fit audience (hobbyists and any small businesses), they had been describing themselves in terms nearly identical to solutions challenging for them to compete with on features and cost. Putting themselves in the same category as a Hubspot led to an expectation mismatch between the visitors to their website and unnecessary comparisons.

Positioning expert, April Dunford, considers choosing the right market category for a product as one of the keys to proper positioning. In her book, *Obviously Awesome*, she explains that people use market categories as a way to mentally organize products. Chosen poorly, the wrong category can confuse your customers. You'll be left fighting an uphill battle with marketing that speaks to a set of assumptions about your product you never intended.

Not having a firm grasp of the job your customers are hiring your product to do can cloud your positioning and, ultimately, the words you're using to convert visitors on your website.

Hesitations

How often have you started filling out an online form and then stopped? Or, you were ready to click the buy button, then suddenly decided not to?

You're not alone. It happens too often. Website users routinely abandon what they're doing at the most critical moment—namely, taking action exactly when it counts most:

- Signing up for an email list
- Putting in credit card details
- Filling out a contact form

Why?

Because the copy needed to reduce whatever friction the user is feeling isn't there. Friction means anything that's making it more difficult for your users to get things done on your site. When we're talking about interactions with your website, friction generally isn't a good thing.

These are typical problems that cause friction:

- Slow page loading times
- Links that don't work
- Poor navigation

Add to that list any copy that does a poor job of addressing your visitors' concerns or potential roadblocks to making a purchase.

What constitutes a hesitation in your customer's mind? This hesitation can be as simple as uncertainty over whether a credit card number is necessary to start a free trial. Imagine reading about an intriguing new online service. The company promises a fourteen-day free trial upon signing up. Except when you get to the bottom of the page to click the button taking you to the sign-up form, there's no telling if there will be any strings attached. If you're not keen on giving up your credit card details, you may decide it's not worth moving on to the next page to find out.

Hesitations can be complex and difficult to tease apart as well. Over the years, I've sifted through thousands of survey responses to questions about uncertainties to purchase. One of the most often provided answers is cost. While this hesitation may seem straightforward, the visitor's concern has less to do with price and more to do with the uncertainty of value. I worked on a project with a subscription business that curated monthly travel deals. Visitors coming to the website along with the company's free-tier customers had a difficult time understanding what they'd get as a premium member and how paying a yearly fee would improve their experience. These people didn't have enough information and messages they found compelling enough to overcome their uncertainty.

This behavior is known as the "ambiguity effect," or the preference to choose an option with a known favorable outcome versus one that is unknown. We're more comfortable making decisions when it's clear what we're getting ourselves into before taking the leap. On a website, providing visitors with the information they need when they need it can go a long way to relieving any hesitation they may have about taking action.

Awareness Level

Whether you're driving down a road or navigating a website, you're looking for signs to tell you where to go and what you can do. Stop signs at intersections and mile markers on highways give us critical information at the right time to help us understand where we are and what we need to know to complete our journey. Without that information, we're lost.

The same holds for the copywriting on websites. Each page must meet the visitor's expectations when they land then provide the ideal progression of messages to make reaching their goals on your site as easy as possible. The key to being able to do that involves knowing about a little something called your prospect's state of awareness.

First introduced and outlined by Eugene Schwartz in his book, *Breakthrough Advertising*, a prospect's state of awareness of their problem, the solutions available, and a brand all play into what words they need to see as they move towards becoming a customer. Schwartz viewed awareness along a continuum across five stages:

1. Most aware: Your prospect is already sold on your product and just needs the facts.
2. Product aware: Your prospect is familiar with your brand, but has not decided if your product is a good fit.
3. Solution aware: Your prospect knows what they want to achieve, but not that you can help her.
4. Problem aware: Your prospect is pretty sure there's a problem, but has no idea if there's a solution.
5. Not aware: Your prospect has no idea about their problem, solution, or anything to do with your brand.

How much convincing you need to do and which argument you have to make, rely heavily on where your prospect is on this continuum. Knowing where your potential customers are on their journey helps you to gauge what they will most likely respond favorably to, making them feel comfortable taking the next step.

The closer your prospects are to being "most aware," the less selling you need to do. They are more inclined to being nudged and taking action. Consider the music streaming service, Spotify, at the top of the awareness scale. When you land on their homepage, you're greeted by the following headline and sub-headline:

Music for Everyone

Millions of song. No credit card needed.

Below these three sentences is a call to action button that says, "Get Spotify Free." That's it. There's no selling, no laundry list of benefits. Why? With over 270 million total active monthly users as of the end of 2019, Spotify has become a household name on par with its top competitor, Apple. They're banking on the fact that the visitors coming to their website not only are highly aware of their brand but ready to sign up.

As you move towards the "completely unaware" end of the scale, you have to spend more time persuading prospects about the relative benefits of your product and how they relate to solving their problem. Take the delivered fresh dog food products on the market as an example. As a dog owner, you may be struggling to find a brand of food to help with your dog's allergies. You know there are more "natural" options; but, you have no idea what those options are or which one might be the best for your pooch. Landing on a homepage like Spotify isn't going to help you out in your decision-making process. You need pains addressed, benefits laid out, features explained along with solid reasons why this pile of food is light years better than the kibble sitting in your pantry.

Think of your prospect's awareness level as the scaffolding for your messaging and copy. When you know your website visitors' relationship to their struggle, solutions available, and your product, you can decide what to put on the page without struggling.

Differentiators

What makes your product stand out in the eyes of your customers? What capabilities does your product have or unique qualities of your offering make it your customers' number one choice? The answers to these questions comprise your differentiators.

Your differentiators are the aspects of your product or service that keep your customers coming back for more and help prospects understand what makes you unique. For our dog food example from above, the product's differentiators may be a combination of ingredients, home delivery, and freshness. Years of experience in a particular niche could be the key differentiator for a freelance copywriter. A fitness app could provide a range of classes and personalized coaching sessions.

Whatever those differentiators are, they're critical in answering that most important of questions popping into your visitors' heads, "Why is this better than the alternatives?" Prospects may be intimately aware of their problems and even have some familiarity with a product, but getting them to choose a new solution can be an uphill battle. Any given product is competing against both the status quo (what prospects are making do with already) and any other comparable solution available. For example, think of customer relationship management or accounting software for small businesses. There are dozens of these subscription software solutions available and alternate ways of handling the books (spreadsheets, Word documents.) Website visitors have one less reason to be pulled into signing up with no way to identify the unique appeal of one over another quickly.

Success

Visitors come to your website for various reasons. They may be searching for answers to questions, to purchase something, or to connect with you. Whatever the reason, they're motivated to do so by a desire to make some sort of progress in their lives. That means your solution needs to not only fix the problem your customers are experiencing, but it has to help them reach their version of the end of the rainbow as well.

Before we dive into what these desired outcomes are, let's take a hot minute to address what they aren't. Contrary to any wishful thinking, copywriting and marketing can't manufacture desired results. Eugene Schwartz shares this insight in *Breakthrough Advertising,* noting the copywriter's job is to "focus those already existing desires onto a particular product." The push to seek out a solution and make life different or better comes from within. The best you can do is connect what's driving your customers with how your product can make those desired outcomes a reality.

What are your customers' desired outcomes? If you're starting to think in terms of the benefits your product or solution offers, you're on the right track. Except most people don't dig deep enough when talking about how their offering can make their customers' lives better. Pull up any random sampling of websites, and you'll notice copy like "Saves time" or "Get more cash in your wallet." Ask just about anyone if they'd like to save time or have more money, and you'll probably get a resounding "Yes!" The problem with not looking beyond these factors is that you miss out on the bigger *why* behind the desire.

Let me give you an example. The way I figure out how to get to the heart of what customers want to happen is to keep asking, "Why?" until there are no more whys left.

For instance, let's say you're selling a weight-loss and exercise program designed specifically for young, college-aged women. Why would these women be interested in your program?

They want to lose weight.

Why do they want to lose weight? Because they want to get rid of the Freshman 15 they put on.

Why do they want to get rid of those fifteen pounds? Because they can't fit into their skinny jeans anymore.

Why do they want to get back into their skinny jeans? Because they feel more attractive and look healthier when they can wear what they want to wear.

Why do they want to feel more attractive and look healthier? Because they will be more confident.

Now we're getting somewhere. The real benefit of your program isn't weight loss; it's confidence-boosting. Here's where the deep-down why comes to light. How customers genuinely want to see their lives improve is the ultimate desired outcome. This expressed desire is what you want to be looking for in the voice of customer research.

There's a method to this messaging madness

In the following chapters, I'll walk you through the best ways to find your customers' struggles, successes, and everything in between. Then we'll look at how they tie together to make your copywriting stronger.

PART II

HOW TO GET YOUR CUSTOMER RESEARCH

3

ASKING YOUR CUSTOMERS AND PROSPECTS THE RIGHT QUESTIONS

Now that you know what elements go into effective messaging, it's time to start planning and conducting some of your research. Ideally, you already have a thriving business with plenty of existing customers and website traffic. If so, you're sitting on a goldmine of potential information to fuel your copywriting.

The key to tapping into that goldmine has everything to do with asking the right questions based on the goal you want and the information you need to learn. That's why we need to take a moment to talk about your research endgame before we dive into the different ways to do your voice in customer research.

Give yourself a head start by defining your goals and objectives

Setting a goal for your research is critically important because it spells out what you're going to do with the data you collect and why. Your goal gives you direction and serves as a constant reminder of what your research needs to achieve.

There are many different goals you can come up with for doing things like surveys or interviews for your business. You may want to know what markets are best to expand into for a particular product or how satisfied your customers are with your support team. Whatever your goal may be, it needs to be specific and tied to a greater purpose for your business.

Otherwise, you may have a difficult time figuring out the steps you need to take to achieve it or how it will provide value to your business as a whole.

For this book, we want to develop surveys and interview questions to gain insights we can use to write more effective copy. How might that translate into a specific goal?

Let's say you're developing a new sales page for an existing high-end product. The current sales page has not been performing as expected. Screen recordings show visitors lingering on the pricing section, spending little time on the rest of the page. Your exit intent survey answers tell you visitors leave without buying because of the cost. You quickly realize there's a disconnect between the product price and the value non-buyers see in the product. You decide to interview your most recent customers to find out why.

Your interview goal might be "to assess how customers perceive the value of XYZ product relative to the costs to write more persuasive copy on the sales page."

With this goal in mind, you are ready to identify your interview objectives. Your objectives consist of the learnings you want to gain from doing your research. These are the bits of information that will help you reach your goal.

You may want to discover answers to the following questions:

- What are customers' biggest hesitations to buying?
- How does the product make customers' lives better?
- What motivated customers to seek out the product?
- What alternatives did our customers use to get the job done before seeking us out?

Once you have your goal and objectives in place, determining what questions to ask will be a whole lot easier because you know what the interview needs to achieve and what you want to learn. The most important thing to remember is that every question should serve the same purpose: to move you closer to reaching your goal.

Conducting surveys by email

You're ready to get answers but not sure where to start. One of the easiest ways to learn from your customers and prospects involves sending your email list a link to a survey. Surveys take little time to set up and minimal to no cost to deploy. While surveys are no substitute for interviews, which allow you to ask follow-up questions and clarify answers, they can give you valuable insights into what a broader swath of people care about most.

Best survey practices

While putting together a survey isn't rocket science, it does require some planning and forethought to get you the best results. Place the following items on your mental checklist while you're working on your next survey.

#1: Keep the number of questions to a minimum

Most people have a limited amount of time, patience, and goodwill when it comes to answering questions. In particular, this applies to email surveys and on-site pop-up surveys. For email surveys, keep the questions limited to a range of six to ten. You'll want your website pop-up surveys to be even shorter, one to two questions max.

From a messaging perspective, you can glean quite a bit of valuable information from a small number of questions. You're not looking for detailed demographics that require dozens of questions and a significant time commitment from your respondents. You're much more likely to see your survey completion rates soar taking a less is more approach.

#2: Stay relevant

Make sure your questions are connected to the task at hand. This item brings us back to knowing what your goal is. Refrain from asking questions just because you'd like to know the answers. If they're not going to serve your direct purposes, leave them out.

For instance, I might ask small business owners what they struggle with the most when writing their website copy. The answers to this question should yield some promising insights to help me write better copy for my book's sales page.

Asking these same people the question "What's your favorite word?" would provide no value. Remember, you're trying to get to the heart of your customer's how and why. If your questions don't lead you down that path, chances are they're not worth asking.

#3: Focus on open-ended questions

When you're looking for copy ideas to swipe from your customers' mouths, you need access to their actual words. Keep yes/no and multiple-choice questions to a minimum. The goal is to get people to express themselves as openly as possible.

Let's say you've created an exercise program for people recovering from back surgery. A useful open-ended question to discover why your recent customers bought your program could be, "What happened after the surgery that pushed you to purchase the program?"

A question like this forces people to think about the circumstances around their choices and gives them more opportunity to elaborate. Suddenly, your customer is telling you not only that she wants to alleviate her back pain but also how that pain is affecting the overall quality of her life (e.g., she can't play with her kids or walk up and downstairs).

Voilà! Your open-ended question has given you a wealth of information about the benefits of your program.

#4: Ditch the bias

Repeat after me, "No leading questions." Don't do things such as including superlatives in your questions. Asking what your respondents think about your bright and cheery website design plants an idea in their heads about the site.

Stay as neutral as possible in your wording to generate the most reliable answers. An example of a neutral question is, "How does reading this copy make you feel?" An example of a biased question looks like, "How does reading this extremely well-researched copy make you feel?" The first question asks without compromising the answer, while the second makes it nearly impossible.

#5: Don't make people think

Steve Krug turned the phrase "Don't make me think!" into a mantra for web designers everywhere. Just like good design and usability on a site, well-crafted questions should be easy to understand. If they are vague or overly complicated, chances are you won't get the answers you're looking for on your first try.

For instance, the question "What types of online copywriting frustrate you the most?" might confuse people. Without including the words to write at the end of the question, respondents might think you're asking them what types of pages are the most frustrating to read.

This type of confusion can lead to you receiving answers that provide little value to your research. Don't ask your survey-takers to tell you *when* they decided to start using your product if you need to know the circumstances affecting their decision-making process. Trust me when I say you'll get time-based answers instead of circumstance-based ones. This situation happened to me after a client changed the wording of just such a question before sending off the survey. I sifted through hundreds of responses, very few helpful in determining how the customers viewed the problem to be solved.

#6: Get people to self-identify whenever possible

Knowing how your prospects and customers think of themselves and the words they use to describe who they are or what they want to do on your site is critically important. For example, a colleague of mine and I wanted to know how the people coming to a client's site classified themselves. We hypothesized that the client's ideal customers and the majority of people coming to his site were beginner programmers, but we weren't sure. My colleague included a question in an initial survey that asked people to choose the term that best described them: *beginner*, *intermediate*, or *advanced.*

It was finding out that the highest percentage of people thought of themselves as beginners helped us tweak the language on the site, so it focused on their needs. A multiple-choice question can work well in this type of situation.

#7: Survey recent customers

When it comes to email surveys, reach out to customers or clients who have bought or worked with you in the last three to six months. Their purchases and your business will still be fresh in their minds. They'll be more likely to remember their experience with you, your product or service, and your website.

It can be helpful to speak with people who have yet to buy from you, too. For example, you may want to understand the challenges they are facing in their businesses and why they have not purchased from you yet. If you can segment your email by prospects, send them their survey with questions tailored to what you're hoping to learn from them.

Examples of questions to ask

So let's get down to brass tacks. Here are some examples of questions I've used in email surveys that tie directly to the Six Elements of Effective Messaging discussed in Part I. The answers have been instrumental in helping me craft more effective copy on various pages, including sales pages.

Consider giving any number of these questions a try in your next survey:

- **"What was happening in your life/business that made you realize you needed a product/service like ours?"** This is a question that will help you define your customers' struggle and give you context for why people seek out your solution.
- **"What problem does our product/service**

lessen or fix for you?" This question can shed light not only on what your customers consider their struggle to be but also the fix. You may find you're solving problems you didn't even know about previously.

- **"What alternatives did you use before buying from/working with us?"** Knowing what types of solutions your customers used instead of yours gives you insight into how they were previously solving their problems. They may have used one solution or jury-rigged several to get the job done.
- **"What concerns or hesitations did you have before you decided to buy from/work with us?"** Addressing any sources of friction around using or buying your product can be the difference between making a sale or not. When you bust hesitations, you give your website visitors fewer reasons to leave.
- **"After you finish your course/working with us/using our product, what personal/professional goal are you hoping to achieve?"** Use this question to help people dig a little deeper into why they sought you out and tap into their desired outcomes.
- "**How aware were you of (the type of products/solutions) before you purchased/signed up for our product/free-trial?"** This particular question lends itself well

to a multiple-choice format. You can give respondents a choice between four options - highly aware, very aware, somewhat aware, and not aware at all. Define each choice by including a description (e.g., researched similar onboarding solutions online.)

This list is just a start. Depending on your circumstances, tweak the questions as needed. Then, test them out.

Noah Kagan's email survey story

In 2013, Noah Kagan of AppSumo started promoting his Monthly1K.com course by emailing 30,000 of his most qualified prospects. The response was dismal. Thirty people out of all of those thousands purchased.

Noah, a phenomenally successful serial entrepreneur, knew how to promote and launch a product online and get results. He was more than a little surprised by the 0.1 percent conversion rate. He jokes about the experience in a blog post where he writes, "I'm Noah Kagan, things always work out for me, right?"

He decided to send a survey to those people who had opened the email, clicked through to the sales page, but chose not to buy. His goal was to figure out what was holding those people back who were interested enough to consider his offer but weren't willing to pull the trigger.

He received a gold mine of information by asking those surveyed to explain why they didn't sign up even if they were interested in the offer. It became apparent that there was not enough information on the sales page to alleviate his prospects' fears about failure in general and using his product in particular.

What did he do? Noah and his team reordered the page to address the most pressing questions people had first, based on the survey. He pulled out the language his prospects were using to talk about starting their businesses and directly used recurring words and phrases in his copy. Plus, he added stories from real users about past failures and the ways the course helped them find success.

The result was an increase in conversions leading to a spike in sales. By asking the right questions of the right people, the answers shed light on what the AppSumo guys were doing wrong with their messaging and gave them a guidepost to making rock-solid changes.

How to get those questions answered

At this point, you should have a good idea of the types of questions to ask in your surveys. Now the trick is getting your customers or prospects to answer them. If you've struggled with your email open rates or survey response rates, you're not alone. The number one complaint I hear people say about asking their customers to complete surveys is, "I can't ever get anyone to respond."

Here are a few tips to improve your survey success with a better email.

#1: Be direct, clear, and don't ask for anything else in the email

It's easy to confuse your email recipients by talking about too many things, then having the call to action to take the survey feels like an afterthought. If you do this, don't be surprised if no one answers your questions. Give your reader one call to action and make the link to your survey highly visible.

Keep your round-up newsletter with multiple links to articles or email about your upcoming course free of appeals to take your survey. Now is not the time to push your customers into the realm of cognitive overload.

#2: Phrase your email subject as a sincere but small request

If you have a good relationship with the people on your email list, many of them will be more than happy to take a few minutes to answer your questions. Try structuring your email subject line as a question, such as, "Can you do me a favor and answer 3 quick questions?"

Letting people know that your request requires only a small commitment of their time, that it serves a purpose, and that their time is highly appreciated and valued, you are giving them fewer reasons to say no in their head.

Also, once people agree to a modest request, getting them to accept a larger one is far more manageable. This type of question is considered getting a "foot in the door," known in the realm of psychology as a compliance/commitment technique. Go for a small yes, and the likelihood of getting a bigger one down the road increases.

#3: Quantify your incentive (if you offer one)

Incentives to take email surveys (e.g., coupons, free downloads, one-on-one sessions) don't always work. The success of this tactic depends on your audience's expectations, their relative needs, and the incentives themselves. With one of my clients, offering the opportunity to win a place in their high-end program for free generated hundreds of thoughtful responses. They have a highly engaged community accustomed to enjoying a multitude of free resources from my client. Another ebook may not have been enough to catch their list's attention.

If you do decide to offer an incentive, make sure to quantify it. Let's say you're offering a free download to an e-book you sell. Don't just say, "Take the survey and get my e-book for free."

If you usually charge $25 for your book, you need to tell your readers the reward for taking the survey is $25. Then, remind them how much $25 is worth—anchor it to something else like paying for a hardback bestseller at full price. Finally, hit on their fear of loss and the fact that if they pass this up, they're essentially throwing away money and learning more about whatever you have to offer.

One last note on incentives: they are not a necessity. I've had B2B software companies send survey requests by email garnering hundreds of responses without the promise of a gift, entry into a drawing, or donation to a charity. I attribute the success more to how well these businesses have nurtured and provided ongoing value to their customers than any single written email. Take a bit of time and assess your current email strategy along with open rates, click-through rates, and response rates before deciding if or what type of incentive is necessary.

#4: Send your email from a real person

Faceless companies don't inspire connection. This lack of humanness applies to your emails as well. Not only should your email be conversational but signed by a real person who works at the company. In some cases, that will be the marketing director. Or, you can include the business owner's name. The particular person is not as important as the gesture. It's a small way to give your customers someone to connect with and respond to personally in your email.

Give this email script a try

Take into consideration the above tips to improve the success of your email campaign, especially tip #1. Remember that most people are extremely busy. Make your email as appealing and user-friendly as possible. That way, you may up your odds of getting those people on your list to answer your survey questions.

Here's a template you can customize and use. I've included two subject lines for those of you who enjoy doing a bit of split testing with your emails.

Subject line #1: Can you do me a favor?

Subject line #2: Do you have 2 minutes to help me out?

Hello [insert name],

I'm working on [insert whatever types of products you design, services you want to sell, or even content you'd like to write] and would appreciate your feedback.

My goal is to *create/design/develop* the kind of *items/services/content* that you can't wait to get your hands on. The best way for me to make sure I'm doing that? You answer a few short and sweet questions.

I know you're busy, so this won't take you more than a couple of minutes.

Click this link: [insert link] to go straight to the survey.

Thanks in advance!

[Your name]

[Your title]

A word about segmentation

Whenever you can segment your email list into clearly defined groups and send your survey to them separately, the better. You'll want to do this for two reasons. Segmentation makes comparing responses between groups so much easier. You'll be able to target those people who are the most appropriate respondents to your questions.

For instance, I put together a survey plan for a client who teaches online courses on how to make iPhone apps. He had an extensive email list of people who purchased on his website, backed one of his courses on Kickstarter, and signed up for his free course. Lumping all of those people together would make it difficult to find out what each group thought about his courses quickly. Presumably, those in the free group would have different expectations of what they should be getting and what they could achieve. Not to mention the fact that his paying customers had proven their willingness to pay. Knowing what made them happy or unhappy helped us key into the messaging that was most important to his highly motivated buyers.

How do you segment your email list? Well, that depends on the third-party email provider you're using. Whether it's MailChimp, Active Campaign, or any number of platforms, each will have its way to go about segmenting lists. Check out their help sections to find out how. The key thing to know is that you can and should be doing this with your list so that when it comes time to talk to different portions of your customer base, you're sending them the most relevant messages. This segmentation includes your surveys.

The power of web and exit surveys

Getting feedback from your existing customers is essential in understanding why people have bought from you in the past and the value they see in what you provide. But that only tells you part of the story. Knowing why potential customers have chosen not to buy, why they decided to abandon your site, or what they're searching for is equally important. (Remember Noah's story?) The reasons given can help you address areas of friction around your offer. One of the best ways to tap into your prospects' behaviors in real-time on your website or landing page is by using web and exit surveys.

What are pop-up surveys?

You can install most pop-up surveys by adding a code snippet generated by a third-party software application to the back end of your website. A small box will pop up in the bottom corner of the page or as a lightbox over the page.

They appear based on preset triggers, such as time on site, traffic source, or activity. For instance, you may find that people are spending a considerable amount of time on your sales page based on your Google Analytics report, but then they bounce off the page. By triggering a one-question survey to pop up before leaving, visitors can tell you why they're not interested.

If you're like most people I talk to, you probably hate pop-ups. Website users complain about pop-ups for several reasons:

- They get triggered before visitors have had a chance to read anything on the site.
- They show up again and again, no matter how many times visitors close them.
- They are notoriously difficult, if not impossible, to close on a mobile phone.

You very well may be cursing them as I write this. Which begs the question, Why bother adding a pop-up if so many people find them annoying?

The simple answer is that they get the job done by learning about why your prospects behave a particular way on your website.

~

Learnings from a page bounce

A simple pop-up question at the right time on one of my client's website pages gave me a critical insight into why their product wasn't selling. The client brought me in to rework the sales page for one of their longtime courses. The first thing I did was dive into their customer research. They had implemented a pop-up survey on this page a few months before another product push. As soon as visitors moved their cursor to exit the page, a small box appeared on the screen with the message, "Tell us why you're leaving."

The client received forty responses. Almost every one of them mentioned price as the biggest roadblock to purchasing the course. Many people talked about their budget as being too small or not being able to see the value the course would bring to their businesses. These visitors had very real hesitations about purchasing that had everything to do with not understanding how the course could fulfill their desired outcomes. *Ouch.* People weren't buying it because they didn't think the course was worth the price. The existing sales page wasn't doing its job, giving visitors all the reasons why the course was an investment in their business they couldn't pass up.

One little pop-up survey gave us a big why behind people leaving the page. We used that information to dig deeper, sending out an email survey to recent customers to get feedback on why they found the course valuable: Bada bing, bada boom. We got a list of benefits straight from the customers to weave into the sales page. The best part was that these benefits came in the customers' own words. In the following chapters, you'll see how you can pull out those words to make your copy perform a whole lot better.

~

Questions to ask in your pop-up surveys

Like any survey, the key to success is knowing the goal you want to achieve before asking questions. To write better-performing copy on your websites and landing pages, you'll need to answer the following questions:

- Does your site meet your visitors' expectations? That is, can they quickly locate what they're

looking for at any given moment? Have they landed in the right place?
- Are there any impediments to your visitors taking action? That is, are there any sources of undue friction, such as being asked to give too much information in a form or not understanding the offer?

In the case of my client's sales page, the goal revolved around determining why visitors weren't buying. We already knew these people qualified as a good source of traffic. We simply needed to know what stopped them from moving to the checkout page. That's why we asked them their reason for leaving.

There are several questions you can ask in your pop-up survey to get the information you need. Consider them variations on the same theme.

When you're interested in identifying who is coming to your site and why, consider asking one of the following questions:

- What's the purpose of your visit today?
- Were you able to find what you were looking for today? (If the answer is no, ask them to tell you what they were hoping to find.)

When you need to know what sources of friction people are encountering on your site, ask one of the following questions:

- Is there anything holding you back from purchasing today? (If the answer is yes, then ask for an explanation.)
- Please tell us why you're leaving today.
- Can we answer any questions before you go? (If the answer is yes, then ask your visitors to list them.)

Getting your pop-up survey questions answered

Response rates for on-site pop-up surveys can be abysmal. Qualaroo, one of the leading companies offering on-site surveys, says that a reasonable response rate for broadly targeted surveys to an entire website average between 5-8 percent. Exit-intent surveys (page-abandonment) tend to be much lower in the 1 percent range.

If you have low traffic numbers, overcoming these percentages can seem daunting. Fear not, there are a few things you can do to increase your chances of getting people to respond. Follow these guidelines when setting up your survey.

#1: Keep the survey simple

You'll want to go down one of two routes: either ask one open-ended question or ask one yes/no question that will lead to an open-ended question asking for an explanation.

#2: Ask the right question at the right time

Think back to what your goal is for this survey. If you want to find out why people abandon their purchases on the checkout page, place your "Why are you leaving?" question there. That may seem like a no-brainer, but you'd be surprised by how many sites ask this question on the home page.

#3: Test how you phrase your questions

What works for one site may not work for another. Your visitors may respond to a question asking essentially the same thing as another, but the way you've worded it is different. The only way to know is to let a question run for a few weeks and see how many responses you're getting in.

A few words about asking one question versus two

You may be wondering about the advantage of asking a yes/no question followed by an open-ended question versus simply asking the open-ended question. Psychology comes into play here. When people take action in a series of steps, they are far more likely to continue down the path they are on. The psychologist and researcher Robert Cialdini dubbed this "commitment and consistency." Persuade people to answer yes to a request, no matter how small, and their need to finish the path they've started on kicks in. Giving your visitors a straightforward yes/no question that requires little thought can be enough to pull them into your survey and get them to provide you with all the details you've wanted to know.

Popping a question after purchase

Consider placing a question on a thank-you page your visitors are directed to after they have purchased something from you or even signed up to your email list. You'll be getting them at the peak of engagement, which makes them primed to answer a question. Here are a few questions to test on your leads and customers:

- What almost stopped you from buying today?
- What convinced you to purchase from us?
- What persuaded you to buy/signup/join?
- What are you most looking forward to learning in this course/newsletter/future emails?

Not only will you gain valuable information to use on your website, but you'll discover insights you can apply to your email campaigns and offers as well.

Email and on-site survey resources

There are plenty of online tools out there, from free to paid versions that you can use for both types of surveys.

Here are a few I like to use when sending surveys by email:

- **SurveyMonkey:** They have both a free and a paid version. The free version allows you to collect an unlimited amount of responses but only view one hundred per survey. This amount will not be enough for larger businesses, but if you are just starting or want to send a very targeted survey by email to only a small segment of your list, it's a good option. Paid plans allow you to take advantage of all the ways Survey Monkey makes it easy to analyze your responses. If you're dealing with a lot of complex data, one of their paid plans is the way to go.
- **Google Forms:** They aren't fancy (although there are some templates to choose from with graphics), but they get the job done and are free to use. Plus, Google does an excellent job of allowing you to synthesize the data/answers into a user-friendly spreadsheet form that you can dump right into Google Sheets.
- **Typeform:** This service has by far the most elegant and versatile types of forms. There is a

cost to unlock your responses unless you use only their core features. If branding and the style of your forms are important to what you're trying to accomplish, this may be the way to go. It's worth checking out.

More and more companies are coming out with online software that can be integrated into your website to perform pop-up surveys. Depending on your needs and traffic, you can go low budget or spend a small fortune each month. Check out the following options:

- **Qualaroo:** By far, the most expensive of the tools, Qualaroo, will be beyond most small businesses' budgets. However, larger enterprises dedicated to ongoing user and voice of customer research may find it worth the expense.
- **Lucky Orange:** This solution provides a range of tools, including on-site polls and surveys, along with heat mapping, recordings, and funnel tracking (just to name a few.) They offer a free trial and then an affordable "Starter" plan.
- **Hotjar:** Like Lucky Orange, Hotjar has a multitude of tools to help you optimize your website, including on-site polls and surveys. The bonus is that they offer a free version.

In the end, the best platform is one you'll use. If you're finding one too confusing or difficult to use, move on.

Phone or online interviews

Having a live conversation with your prospects and customers can give you insights that simply aren't possible from asking survey questions. When you talk with someone, you're able to ask follow-up questions and encourage the person to give you more details.

As with your surveys, you'll want to target existing customers who have worked with you or bought from you within the last six months and your prospects who have yet to purchase from you. The most effective way to do that is to reach out to those who have previously shown interest in talking to you. Those will be the people who have sent you emails in the past thanking you for answering their questions, telling you how great your product is, or even hiring you again.

Also, consider analyzing your email list. Providers like MailChimp show you who on your list opens your emails and with what kind of frequency. Pull out the top ten or twenty people who are the most engaged with your emails as candidates to reach out to in the future.

Tip: Start creating email swipe files. Every time you receive an email from a customer or prospect with praise or feedback, place it in an email folder. Give each folder a name that corresponds to the content inside (e.g., Customer Thank-You Notes, Customer Questions). Over time, you'll accumulate a list of highly motivated people to contact when you need feedback and a nifty little storehouse of words to mine for later research.

Getting the interview

Send an email similar to the one asking for a response to your survey. The same rules apply. Keep it short, sweet, and conversational in tone. Let the person know why you're interested in talking to him or her, how long you expect the conversation to last, and where you'd like the conversation to take place (e.g., on the phone or via conferencing software).

Fifteen to twenty minutes is barely enough time to create a rapport with someone so that you can get meaty answers to your questions. In an ideal world, you'd want to set aside at least forty-five minutes for an interview. The problem is that most people aren't willing to commit that much time to an interview. You run the risk of getting hardly any yes responses. That's why I suggest asking for no more than thirty minutes and making the most of it.

Tip: Link to an online scheduler in your email. These schedulers are third-party applications that allow people to choose from open times on your calendar. Less back and forth over email, attempting to find a mutually convenient time for both of you, means you are more likely to get that interview booked.

Questions to ask in your interview

Think of your interviews as less of a Q&A and more of a conversation. Your goal is to find out as much as you can about the why behind their actions. You need to ask those open-ended questions, listen, then follow up to see if you can get the person to elaborate further.

After asking a few basic questions about the person's background or business, you'll want to ask questions that focus on the behaviors driving their decision-making process along with the circumstances around those behaviors. These types of questions will help you tap into the actions your prospects and customers take when seeking solutions to their problems.

Why is this strategy so important? As humans, we are notoriously good at saying one thing and doing another. "Do as I say, not as I do," my brother would tell me when I was a kid. This advice applied to things like taking out the trash and going to bed early. Fast forward several decades and the same holds for me now. Ask me what I want to be eating for dinner, and I'll tell you, "A healthy stir fry with a potpourri of nutritious grains." Ask me what I ate for dinner last night and why I made that choice, you may get a very different answer (think frozen vegetable pizza after a long day.) Understanding what people want and how they feel only provides helpful information within the context of their actions.

Below you'll find some questions you can use as jumping-off points for your interviews to make getting to that "why" a little easier:

- How has using my product/hiring me improved your business/life? What have you been able to achieve or accomplish?
- What kind of experience have you had using the product/working with me?
- What were the problems you were facing in your business/life that led you to my product/solution?
- What made you realize the old way of operating wasn't working?
- How did you solve these problems in the past? What sorts of solutions were you using before my product or hiring me?
- What alternatives did you consider using/hiring before deciding on my product/service?
- Why did you choose my product/solution over the other options?
- Was there anything that almost held you back from purchasing from me/hiring me?

Listen to their responses and, whenever possible, move the conversation forward by asking them to elaborate not only on the circumstances around their actions but how those actions made them feel. In doing so, you'll start to get a complete picture of how your product or solution fits into your customers' lives.

Do I really need to interview people?

Interviewing people can be intimidating and time-consuming. Not everyone wants to do it. You can get a wealth of information from all the other sources I outline in this book without ever doing an interview. However, I suggest setting aside time to talk to at least five of your prospects or customers. If you manage to book only two interviews, take what you can get. Think of this as your opportunity to connect with those people most interested in what you have to offer. If nothing else, you might find answers to questions you didn't even know you had.

Record your interviews

The best way to keep track of what's being said in an interview is to record it. Taking notes can work, but remember that the goal here is to get the words verbatim that your prospects or customers are saying. It can be challenging to stay focused on the person you're talking to while writing everything down. Consider using screen-recording software for conference calls or call-recording software if talking on the phone. Both will allow you to make a recording of the conversation, which you can then have made into a transcript. Always tell the person you're interviewing that they're being recorded and get their permission.

Email script: Get people to respond to your interview request

Here is another email template that you can use and customize. Once again, I've included two subject lines for you to test and tweak.

Subject line #1: Quick question for you, [person's name]

Subject line #2: I'd love to chat with you

Hey [person's name],

I'm doing some research on [insert whatever types of products you design, services you want to sell, or even content you'd like to write] and am asking a few of my [recent clients, customers] if they're willing to jump on a 30-minute call with me.

There's no sales pitch, just looking for your thoughts on [insert what you want to talk about.]

If you're game, click here to pick a time that works best for you.

Thanks,

[Your name]

Other ways to learn what your customers have to say

There are several different places you can find answers to your questions without creating a survey, sending an email, or picking up the phone. Use these sources to fill in any gaps you need to fill from your primary sources (surveys and interviews.)

Testimonials

If you've been in business for some time, you will likely have several testimonials from past clients. Hopefully, these will already be sitting on your website for prospective customers to see. Or, you'll have them in emails sent to you. Either way, they can be a terrific resource for words and phrases that tap into why people love what you do.

Live chat or email customer support logs

If you're a business that uses either a live chat on your website or customer support by email, you should have records that document your correspondence with customers. These are phenomenal resources for discovering what questions and concerns are cropping up for your existing customers. They can be extremely helpful for understanding bugs in your system or problems with your product, too.

Blog comments

Sometimes your blog posts will create even more questions than answers for your visitors. Don't look at that as a negative. Every question that crops up is an opportunity to understand more about your customers. The comments section can also be a goldmine for people expanding on how they feel about a topic. Remember, in Chapter 1, how I said that digging into feelings gets you closer to the real motivations behind why people want to purchase? Depending on how active your readers are in the comments section and how much they enjoy interacting with you there, you may hit pay dirt when you go to message mine.

Social media comments

Take a look at your various social media channels for comments by fans or customers. Often, you can find powerful mini testimonials in the form of tweets or Facebook comments. These short snippets can give you an idea of what your fans rave about and the words they use to do so.

Final thoughts on pulling together your customer research

Conducting customer research, whether it's for product development or website optimization, takes work. It's easy to get bogged down. You may find yourself falling into one too many rabbit holes, thinking you need more and more information to get the job done when, in fact, you don't.

Consider what your goals are for your copy and your website. Getting ten interviews and hounding your email list for months to answer survey questions may not be worth your time or your email subscribers' patience. Before you start creating surveys and lining up interviews, take a look at the customer research, you do have that has been hiding in plain sight: existing survey responses, testimonials, tweets from raving fans. Set them aside, and we'll get back to them in Chapter 5 when we talk about pulling out key messages in your copy.

4

HOW TO DO CUSTOMER RESEARCH WITHOUT THE CUSTOMERS

What happens when you're just starting or don't have loads of customers eager to respond to your survey questions? You can still do customer research to help your website copy. You just have to be a little more creative with how you go about it. I'll let you in on the best trick of the trade, which I keep in my back pocket at all times. It's called review mining, and I learned it straight from the queen of conversion copywriting, Joanna Wiebe of CopyHackers.

What is review mining?

Review mining is the process of pulling out the most compelling snippets of copy you can find from reviews of products or services similar to yours (we'll get into exactly how you do it in the next chapter). You start by spending some quality time on places like Amazon, Yelp, or Etsy, trolling through the review sections. Your goal is to learn as much as possible about the hesitations, needs, and motivations of real-life customers so you can plug that right into your copy.

I've gone through this process for many clients, from software companies to stationery designers. And it all starts the same way. I begin by brainstorming the best places to look for commentary by consumers. Where you mine depends entirely on what you're selling. For instance, let's say you have developed a line of non-toxic cleaning products with all-natural ingredients. By typing the words *eco-friendly cleaning products* into the Amazon search bar, you'll get thousands of entries to peruse. Most have multiple reviews with people openly discussing what their likes and dislikes are in black and white.

Sounds pretty easy, right? And it is, most of the time. When you can find a tangible product that's comparable to yours in every way, you may be able to make Amazon your one-stop-shop for voice of customer mining. Some products have hundreds of reviews, keeping you busy for hours.

But what if you're trying to find out what people think about a service that doesn't lend itself to online reviews? Or if you're selling a product that's relatively new to the marketplace? Suddenly, knowing what to search for isn't so straightforward.

What to do when you don't know where to look

Instead of focusing on what you're selling, shift your thinking to the outcomes your prospects want to achieve. Even if you don't have your customer feedback to draw on, you probably have a good idea of what people want from you. Your product or service solves a particular problem. Your first step is to identify that problem and stick a pin in it.

Once you've pinned down what you believe to be your prospect's biggest problem, ask yourself this question:

If I was trying to solve [insert your prospect's problem], where would I look online to find the answers?

When you think in terms of where your ideal customers might search for solutions, you'll have an easier time finding the places where they may be hanging out talking about it.

A real-world example from the research trenches

Several years ago, a digital design agency came to me, asking for help with their messaging. The guys at the agency decided it was about time to put together a solid value proposition for their home page and had someone rewrite their signature marketing piece. They had a handful of testimonials for me to look at, but no surveys or interviews.

How tough could this be? I thought. *There's a ridiculous amount of people talking about website design and development. No problem.*

Once I started digging in, I found it was a problem. Why? Finding the words spoken by clients about their concerns, needs, and desires when it came to hiring a design agency proved far more complicated than I'd anticipated. Going on forums to see what designers and developers had to say about their jobs and reading book reviews on Amazon about web design wasn't going to cut it.

After spending far too much time coming up with a big fat zero through my research, I took a deep breath and asked myself this: *If I needed to hire a digital design firm and wanted to know the advantages and avoid the pitfalls, what would I search for online?*

Suddenly, my mindset shifted, instead of the question revolving around *where* it became *what.* I didn't go to my usual hunting grounds like Amazon or Quora first but started with a good old Google search. I put in long-tail keyword searches like *digital agency client questions*, *hiring mobile app developers*, and *UX designer skills*. I found articles in online business magazines that discussed what motivated businesses (similar to those attracted to my client) hire agencies, written by the people doing the hiring. Even better, an article cropped up about what digital agency clients say in private, filled with quotes tapping into clients' most significant objections.

While I didn't have the words of my client's customers, I had the next best thing—words from other people's customers. And that was enough to help fill the gaps.

~

Looking beyond reviews

The previous example illustrates that you can find people talking about comparable products and services in places other than reviews. When you are forced to think outside the box and mine alternative sources, start by asking yourself what problem your customers need to solve, then think about where they would go online for the answer. Look to blog comments and forums in particular when you want to find the words people use to define what they struggle with most.

Here are several other places to search for gold:

- **Community forums:** Try searching for the problem your product or service solves, and include the word *forum* in your search.
- **Reddit:** This site contains forums called "subreddits" on just about every subject imaginable.

- **Quora:** Go here to find answers to just about any question. Search for a product or topic, and you'll find people writing about it.
- **Competitor blog posts and testimonials:** Look at the comment section of blog posts and the testimonials on competitor sites. These can give you clues about what questions and praise people have for your competitors.
- **G2 and Capterra:** These sites provide aggregated reviews for software companies. Capterra has a pros and cons section in each review, perfect for learning what users love and revile in a piece of software. G2 asks the questions, "What do you like best?" and "What do you dislike?" While less than probing questions, they provide a jumping-off point for reviewers to discuss the software's most-used features and difficulties.

Surveying like-minded customers

Even if you don't have your customers, you can ask people's questions in your target audience through a service like Survey Monkey or Pollfish. Both of these companies allow you to create pay-per-response surveys and send them to a network of people based on criteria you define.

While not exactly cheap, surveying people in your target audience has its advantages for your messaging research. As I mentioned in the last chapter, mining chat logs and social media comments can be constructive for rounding out your voice of customer research; but, it's best used to fill in the gaps. The same holds for review mining without the customers. With a survey that taps into a large sample size, you can quickly get a more solid handle on prioritizing messages. You're not relying only on a handful of reviews that may or may not represent your solution to set the direction of your copy.

What questions should you ask in a pay-per-response survey? They will be very similar to what you'd ask your existing customers. For example, let's say you've created an app to automate check-ins at doctors' offices. To find out what administrative staff considers their most significant problem when patients arrive for a doctor's appointment, you may ask, "What do you find difficult about how you currently handle the patient check-in process?" Use the example survey questions from the last chapter to give you ideas on where to start.

Keeping track of your online sources

As soon as you start searching online for places to mine, make sure you have a system in place so you can refer back to your sources easily. This system will be vital once you start digging into the various review sites, blogs, and forums.

There are multiple ways to go about keeping track of your sources. You can go the spreadsheet or Word/Google document route, copying and pasting the URLs onto a page. While that's a far better alternative to keeping bookmarks saved in your browser, consider using a bookmarking application instead.

My two favorite tools are Evernote and Notion. Think of them as your online filing systems. In Evernote, you can create notebooks and then individual notes to stick in them. Those notes can include links to web pages and tags to make searching for the content more accessible. Notion allows you to save links and catalogs them as well, but their file system capability is unique. You can create blocks of content, group them onto a table, and then quickly move them around to see how every idea relates to the other.

No matter which tool you choose to use, take time to set aside a few minutes to put a bookmarking system in place before you start Internet-surfing. I suggest creating either a table in Notion or an Evernote notebook devoted solely to your message-mining project. From there, categorize or tag each link source. The point is to make your resources easy to find, so you don't waste valuable time hunting for a link you've already seen.

PART III

ANALYZING YOUR RESEARCH

5

GET YOUR MESSAGING DUCKS IN A ROW

You've asked your customers and prospects questions. You've figured out the best places to learn where people are seeking out solutions like yours and what they are saying about them. Now what? How do you take all those survey responses, interviews, and bookmarked web pages and decide what will be the most helpful for your copy?

Compile customer quotes and categorize by messaging element

Go through your survey responses and all those reviews and comments you bookmarked online one by one (yes, don't skip any because you never know when you might come across a compelling insight, you can drop into your copy word for word). You're looking for phrases that correspond to one of those six elements of effective messaging covered in Chapter 2.

These phrases will do one of the following things:

- Reference the respondents' biggest pain points
- Tell you what triggered the respondents to seek out a solution
- Key into the respondents' hesitations or concerns about purchasing
- Help you understand respondents' awareness level
- Identify what makes your solution special/different compared to others in the respondents' eyes
- Tell you what success looks like to respondents

There are numerous ways you can keep track of these customer quotes. Again, it's a matter of deciding what tool works best for you and how dividing the information collected makes the most sense. I've found it useful to set up separate spreadsheets or documents for each resource (e.g., survey, interview, reviews, etc.) that includes headings for the messaging elements. That way, you can easily place pulled quotes under the appropriate heading while keeping track of where each quote came from online.

Let's take a look at how to identify the words and phrases by messaging elements.

Struggle

Think of your customers' struggles or pain points in terms of the driving forces behind seeking you out. If you conducted a survey, you'd want to look at the responses to any questions about how they view the problem to be solved and what compelled them to search for a product or solution like yours. *Example: "...trying to find a pair of jeans that look flattering and feel comfortable shouldn't be so hard."*

The Fix

You'll find the fix your solution needs to accomplish embedded within the context of how your customers attempt to overcome their struggles. Look for places where your customers or prospects talk about what spurred them to find a solution to their problems. Their actions will give you insights as to what event or series of events made them recognize they have a problem and what job your solution must get done for them. *Example: "After spending hours searching online for caterers, florists, and photographers for my wedding, I felt overwhelmed with all the choices. I needed someone to give me the pros and cons and just spell out my options." Or "I used to hunt for a healthy snack on my lunch break that filled me up, and I could take on the run."*

Hesitations

Pull out phrases that give you details about why people considered not buying, signing up, or moving forward into your funnel. You're looking for voiced anxieties that hold your visitors back from taking action on your website. These phrases will help you understand if you need more copy to alleviate concerns or if you need to modify your existing copy. *Example: "I'm not sure if I have to give my credit card information to sign up for the free trial." Example: "I don't understand which plan is the best fit for my needs."*

Awareness Level

If you've sent out a survey that included a multiple-choice question about your customers' state of awareness (see Chapter 3 for a suggested question), you'll get a good idea where your customers sit on the awareness spectrum without additional message mining. When you don't have many customers, website traffic, or people on your email list, you'll need to dig into your interviews and any supplemental review mining to learn as much as you can about their awareness level. Look for any content that gives you an indication of the familiarity with your brand, your solution, or solutions similar to yours. *Example: "I've been researching a tool that makes automating my scheduling online easier, so I can stop wasting time with all the back and forth emails."*

Differentiators

Search for the phrases that signal what your customers love or rave most about when it comes to your product or service. Remember, these are the things that your customers consider your "X-Factor" to be, not you. These differentiators may overlap, but we're most concerned with what sets you apart from your competitors in your customers' eyes. *Example: "... nowhere else have I found an at-home hair coloring product that makes my hair look like I just came from the salon."*

Success

These are the phrases and sentences that will tell you what your prospects want your product or solution to achieve for them - aka their desired outcomes. Your customers' success is tied to how your product has made their lives better. Outside of survey and interview responses, look for these desired outcomes in success stories, testimonials, and case studies. *Example: "I'm interested in becoming more competitive in my niche with the skills from this course." or "Your custom logo designs have made my brand look so professional I finally feel like people will take me seriously when they come to my site."*

THINK of these six elements as buckets where you can dump the various pulled quotes for later analysis. Don't worry about how they all fit together at this point. Once you've gone through any bookmarked online resources, surveys, and interview responses, you'll be ready to pull apart the contents of each bucket for assessment.

List frequently used words

Along with pulling out phrases and sentences, you'll want to keep a running tally of individual words that repeat. Open a new document, and start copying and pasting in it the words you notice multiple people using to describe your product or solution, how it makes them feel, or what prompted them to seek you out in the first place. Add a tick mark each time the same word appears in a response. Once done, rearrange the list from most used to least used.

Is this a tedious exercise? Why, yes, yes, it is. Can you skip it? You can, but I'd recommend you don't. Here's why. This exercise is a simple way of providing you with an at-a-glance priority list of words to plug into your copy and helping you tap into the mindset of your customers.

~

Paint a picture of your customers with the words they use

Fear, confidence, frustration, and self-doubt were a few of the top recurring words pulled from a message-mining exercise for a recent client. You might expect these words to show up in comments about online dating or searching for a job, not learning how to market yourself better as a photographer. But this is what I found both from the client's customer survey responses and sifting through relevant blog and forum comments.

The more I read, the more tally marks these words received. Many respondents and commenters felt consumed by fear and frustration when it came to talking about themselves during their search for answers to solve their business marketing problems. They were having a tough time turning a profit, and feeling their work was valued.

Between the frequently used words on my list and the customer quotes, it became clear the group searching for a solution like the one my client offered needed strategies they felt confident would work and help them feel supported. This lack of objective proof was precisely where the copy on my client's course sales page missed the mark. The words on the page neglected to spell out exactly how gaining the skills from the course could alleviate the genuine pain these people were feeling. The fact that the page didn't overcome these objections meant visitors to the page had a difficult time understanding the value of taking the course and whether the person selling it understood their needs. By simply asking a few targeted questions, we learned the key reasons why prospects weren't buying and how they described the biggest roadblocks to success in their businesses.

~

The FAQs of voice of customer research

Once you start this process for the first time, you're bound to have questions. Each time I've written or spoken about some parts of this process, a new query pops up. So let's tackle the most obvious, along with a couple you might not have considered.

How many survey responses or reviews do I need to mine?

There's no set number. More is better when it comes to sifting through this kind of qualitative research. Reading two or three reviews and a handful of survey responses may not give you a representative view of what's most important to your customers. It may skew your assessment of what messages you should focus on when you sit down to write.

Message mining is not the place to cut corners. Aim to read through all your survey and interview responses. If you're supplementing your customer responses with things like Amazon reviews, shoot for at least ten to twenty to mine. If you're relying on outside sources

(Amazon, Yelp, forums, etc.) for your research, make twenty your starting point.

What if I have thousands of open-ended survey responses? Do I have to go through all of them?

You will hit a point of diminishing returns. I cap the number between 150 and 200. I've found that enough repetition crops up after a few hundred responses. Reading through more is unnecessary. You'll be able to pull out the key themes and customer quotes that are worth sticking directly in your copy while saving yourself time.

If you have more responses, by all means, read through them. You might find a particularly well-said comment that sums up how a majority of your customers are feeling. The point is you should be able to get what you need without reading the equivalent of a Tolstoy novel.

What if no one will respond to my requests for interviews or surveys?

If you've made multiple attempts to engage with your prospects and customers and you're getting no response, continuing to reach out may very well only irritate them. I suggest sending out the first email and giving people at least five days to respond. If you haven't received a response by that time, send a quick follow-up email that reminds them of your request with a way to take action. After two to three appeals, stop. Dive into the review mining and do your best to find out what other businesses' customers are saying.

How do I know what's worth copying and pasting into my document?

There's no way around it. You'll have to make some judgment calls. Not every comment you read will either provide much insight or sound particularly compelling. For instance, "I loved it!" doesn't tell you a whole lot. If you find dozens of people using the word *love* to describe how they feel about your product or solution, note how often that word appears (as described previously). Forget adding the rest of the sentence to one of your categories.

Refer back to the descriptions for each of the six elements and the examples I provided. As you get more practiced at pulling copy from your research, you'll have an easier time figuring out what makes sense to keep.

If I have plenty of primary customer research (surveys or interviews), is it necessary to look at reviews or comments about other products or solutions?

No, it's not necessary. If you've met your goals with the questions, you've asked and received a slew of meaningful responses, mine what you have. The benefit of looking to outside resources is comparing how your competitors' customers view their offerings. Are their customers raving about a particular feature you didn't think was important? Do their customers express hesitations about buying that mirror or seem in opposition to your own customers' comments? Additional mining puts your messaging into a broader context and helps you see where your competition may be failing or doing exceptionally well.

Consider this process an exercise in data triangulation

This type of messaging research can seem a bit squishy at times. You're not dealing in quantifiable numbers or absolutes. As the researcher, messaging strategist, and copywriter, you have to assess what your customers need to see on the page - even if you don't get as many interviews, survey responses, or reviews to mine as you'd like. That's why we pool multiple data sources to get a complete picture of what messages show up repeatedly.

Don't worry about reaching a magical number of data points. Instead, focus on thoughtfully teasing apart the information you have, looking for points of convergence. You'll gain enough valuable insights into your customers to set your website copy up for success.

6

DETERMINING YOUR KEY MESSAGES

Now that you've pulled out and categorized the most insightful phrases and sentences from your customers, you're ready to start analyzing what you have.

Think of this process going forward to distill all of those words, phrases, and sentences and put them into a usable priority list of messages for your website. In this chapter, we're going to focus on putting together a messaging cheat sheet that you'll keep by your side when you move on to tackling the copy on your website.

It's where you'll plot out the messages your buyers care about, keep track of the most compelling quotes, and document your critical insights into your buyer's mindset.

Sift through your buckets to find the top messages

The first place to start is with the customer quotes that you categorized in Chapter 5. You'll want to focus on one category at a time. Think in terms of recurring themes as you read through each quote. The goal is to find the top messages your prospects or customers are saying and prioritize them based on how often they appear. To do that, you'll need to summarize each of the recurring messages you find and then note how many times they repeat.

For example, let's say you develop online health coaching programs for women. You're looking at the quotes you placed in the "Success" column after mining all your research. You find two similar messages spoken by two separate women:

"I don't want to spend my days worrying about my body image."

"I'd love to take my kids swimming in public this summer and feel confident wearing my swimsuit."

While they say something different, the desired outcome motivating them to seek out a fix is the same: feeling comfortable with how they look. You'll want to create a summary description of that one message (e.g., body image discomfort) and keep track of how many times you come across customers expressing it.

You may notice a particular message showing up only once, while others crop up multiple times. That's okay. You simply want to distill those messages so that you have a workable list to prioritize.

Priority Messages List

Create a table with a column on the left labeled, Message Bucket, and a column on the right labeled, Prioritized Messages (Most Referenced to Least.) Place the six elements in the left column with their corresponding top messages in the right.

For our women's online health coaching business, here's what the summarized messages might look like in order of priority for each of the key messaging elements.

Struggle

What's the struggle to be resolved or the pain overcome with the help of your solution?

- Not able to find a sustainable program
- Tired of one-size-fits-all programs
- No program fits my lifestyle
- Too much conflicting information

The Fix

What's the job your solution needs to get done?)

- Takes the guesswork out of nutrition/exercise
- Focuses on fitness and healthy eating, not just losing weight
- Provides built-in accountability from a community of like-minded women

Hesitations

What makes your ideal customers worry about taking action?

- Afraid this will be another program that fails
- Ability to sustain motivation
- Getting enough support and accountability
- Is there a money-back guarantee?

State of awareness

How aware are your ideal customers of their problem or your solution?

Product aware - Prospects are aware of your brand, has tried other solutions but doesn't know why your brand is better than the rest.

Differentiators

What's enticing about your solution that makes it the right fit for your customer?

- Fully customized programs based on each woman's needs

- Woman-only focused
- One-on-one support from a certified coach

Success

How is life better after using your solution? What does success look like?

- Increased confidence in body image
- Improved health with balanced nutrition and exercise
- Feels stronger and fitter

Message Bucket	Prioritized Messages *(Most Referenced to Least)*
Struggle *What's the struggle to be resolved or the pain overcome with the help of your solution?*	• Not able to find a sustainable program • Tired of one-size-fits-all programs • No program fits my lifestyle • Too much conflicting information
The Fix *What's the job your solution needs to get done?*	• Takes the guesswork out of nutrition/exercise • Focuses on fitness and healthy eating, not just losing weight • Provides built-in accountability from a community of like-minded women
Hesitations *What makes your ideal customers worry about taking action?*	• Afraid this will be another program that fails • Ability to sustain motivation • Getting enough support and accountability • Is there a money-back guarantee?
State of awareness *How aware are your ideal customers of their problem or your solution?*	Product aware - prospects are aware of your brand, has tried other solutions but doesn't know why your brand is better than the rest
Differentiators *What's enticing about your solution that makes it the right fit for your customer?*	• Fully customized programs based on each woman's needs • Woman-only focused • One-on-one support from a certified coach
Success *How is life better after using your solution? What does success look like?*	• Increased confidence in body image • Improved health with balanced nutrition and exercise • Feels stronger and fitter

Priority messages by element bucket in table form

After going through the pulled quotes in each category, you may find that you have more than the above example does. Or you may realize that you're quickly filling your list of hesitations but struggling to get more than two on your differentiators' list. It all depends on the amount of mining you did upfront and what came out of your customers' and prospects' mouths.

Remember, the whole point of this process is to find out what people think and the words they use to express themselves. Don't be tempted to add items to the list that you believe should be there.

Identify your top ten most compelling customer quotes

I hope you didn't think we would toss out all of those quotes you worked so hard to mine. Those phrases and sentences are going to come in handy when you're ready to write your copy.

We'll get into the how in the next section, but right now, your task is to make a list of your top ten. Go into your existing documents with all of your customer quotes and place an asterisk next to your top ten, or copy and paste them into a separate document. These top ten quotes can be from any of the three categories, but your focus should be on the ones that match at least one of the following criteria.

Particularly insightful

These sentences and phrases get straight to the heart of how your customers view their problems or your solution. They do it in a way that may not have occurred to you before or seemed obvious. *Example: "I can be my own biggest obstacle to getting the results I want."*

Well said or summed up a point nicely

Sometimes you'll come across a line that perfectly captures the tone and sentiment of what many of your customers are trying to say. These are the gems that are worth highlighting and testing out in your copy. *Example: "I don't want to just turn heads with my designs. I want to make them spin."*

What people rave about

Knowing the words your customers use when they're talking about how much they love your work helps you write about what makes your business unique or attractive. *Example: "You bring the whole process of making widgets to life with colorful, detailed graphics and videos filled with examples."*

Map your customer's mindset

After taking all this time to gather your research, distill the messages, and pull out the most compelling customer quotes, your next step is to conclude what makes your customers tick and how you'll go about using that knowledge to tailor the copy on your site. Think of this step as the intersection where your customers' thoughts meet your business's offerings.

The following is a Customer Mindset Analysis example based on the imaginary coaching business we've been using. Like the Priority Messages List, create a table to make the information easily accessible. The left-hand column will mirror those six categories you've come to know so well. The right-hand side will summarize what's going on in your customers' minds, based on your cumulative knowledge of the research you've done, and lists what you'll want to include in your copy.

How does your business solve your customers' problems?

(Struggle + Fix)

There's a tremendous amount of overwhelming information for these women. They don't know who to trust or follow. They know losing weight, eating healthier, and looking after their own needs takes work; but without the reassurance that they can achieve results with a program tailored to them, they're reluctant to try another. Customers need access to health and fitness coaching with built-in accountability that fits their schedule.

Focus the copy on:

- Easy to access, online programs customized to each person
- Simple to follow exercises and nutrition information

- The accountability aspect of others in the program
- Testimonials from other women who have seen great results

What doubts get in the way of becoming a customer?

(Hesitations)

This isn't many of these women's first rodeo when it comes to eating healthier or improving how they take care of themselves. They're worried they will sink money into yet another course or training program that doesn't fulfill its promises.

Focus the copy on:

- Position offerings as an investment, not an expense
- Spell out the value coaching provides—tangible and intangible things they will get out of it
- Highlight how the sign-up process and guarantees work
- Give objective and social proof, including how many women coached, testimonials from experts

Where is your prospect in the decision-making process?

(State of Awareness)

These prospects are acutely aware of their problems, other solutions on the market, and have familiarity with the brand. However, they have doubts about the program fitting their needs and how it compares to others like it on the market.

Focus the copy on:

- How this program is different/better than other similar online programs
- Comparing/contrasting life before and after the program, making sure to mention why those other programs didn't lead to success

What do customers love/rave about? What's the pull?

(Differentiators)

Customers are drawn to the customizable nature of the program, supportive community, and expertise of the coach. As prospects are "product" aware, they require less copy outlining the pains or struggles and more copy helping visitors understand the unique value of this particular program. See above on where to focus the copy.

What are the customers' desired outcomes? What's the internal push?

(Success)

Women interested in an online health coaching program want guidance and support that focuses on helping them become healthier while learning to love themselves in the process. While they understand there aren't any quick fixes, they want to make sure that whatever program they join will lead to increased emotional and physical wellbeing.

Focus the copy on:

- Tangible and intangible benefits gained from the program (e.g. pounds lost, confidence gained)
- Program features tied directly to benefits

How does your business solve your customers' problems? ***(Struggle + Fix)***	There's a tremendous amount of overwhelming information for these women. They don't know who to trust or follow. They know losing weight, eating healthier, and looking after their own needs takes work; but without the reassurance that they can achieve results with a program tailored to them, they're reluctant to try another. Customers need access to health and fitness coaching with built-in accountability that fits their schedule. Focus the copy on: • Easy to access, online programs customized to each person • Simple to follow exercises and nutrition information • The accountability aspect of others in the program • Testimonials from other women who have seen great results
What doubts get in the way of becoming a customer? ***(Hesitations)***	This isn't many of these women's first rodeo when it comes to eating healthier or improving how they take care of themselves. They're worried they will sink money into yet another course or training program that doesn't fulfill its promises. Focus the copy on: • Position offerings as an investment, not an expense • Spell out the value coaching provides—tangible and intangible things they will get out of it • Highlight how the sign-up process and guarantees work • Give objective and social proof, including how many women coached, testimonials from experts
Where is your prospect in the decision-making process? ***(State of Awareness)***	These prospects are acutely aware of their problems, other solutions on the market, and have familiarity with the brand. However, they have doubts about the program fitting their needs and how it compares to others like it on the market. Focus the copy on: • How this program is different/better than other similar online programs • Comparing/contrasting life before and after the program, making sure to mention why those other programs didn't lead to success
What do customers love/rave about? What's the pull? ***(Differentiators)***	Customers are drawn to the customizable nature of the program, supportive community, and expertise of the coach. As prospects are "product" aware, they require less copy outlining the pains or struggles and more copy helping visitors understand the unique value of this particular program. See above on where to focus the copy.
What are the customers' desired outcomes? What's the internal push? ***(Success)***	Women interested in an online health coaching program want guidance and support that focuses on helping them become healthier while learning to love themselves in the process. While they understand there aren't any quick fixes, they want to make sure that whatever program they join will lead to increased emotional and physical wellbeing. Focus the copy on: • Tangible and intangible benefits gained from the program (e.g. pounds lost, confidence gained) • Program features tied directly to benefits

Customer Mindset Analysis in table form

It's all about connecting the dots

The customer mindset analysis exercise forces you to pump those mental muscles and tie what drives your customers' behavior directly to how you'll need to write about what you're selling. Each takes into account the elements of effective messaging and then provides a hypothesis for what sort of copy will be required to address specific, recurring messages.

If you're wondering whether there's some overlap between rows, you'd be correct. In our previous example, some of what the potential customer sees as her problem is also what fuels her doubts and hesitations. Not being able to find a coach who will tailor a program to her lifestyle and needs is a problem that gives her pause to hit that "buy" button or could cause her to become a lead on another mailing list. Your copy solution to address both that pain and the hesitation could be a testimonial—or several.

Once you start looking at your business and its products or services from a customer's perspective, you can begin to see where your copy needs to fill the gaps.

What to do next

Create three documents or spreadsheets. You can refer back to the two tables in this chapter to help you organize your priority messages and customer mindset analysis:

- **Priority messages:** A list of the most recurring messages in each of the four customer quote categories
- **Top ten most compelling quotes:** Particularly well-said or insightful comments or what people are raving about
- **Customer mindset analysis:** A summary of your findings, along with how your copy can address them

Once you've done the hard work of filling these in, you'll be ready to write your copy.

Go to www.makementionmedia.com/resources to get these document templates.

PART IV

APPLYING WHAT YOU'VE LEARNED TO YOUR WEBSITE COPY

7

IT'S TIME TO TALK ABOUT YOU

If you've gone through all the steps to gather your voice of customer research, mine it, and analyze it, pat yourself on the back. You're light-years ahead of most businesses, big and small. Unlike business owners who set out to build a better mousetrap and market it without any clue about what their customers are thinking, you've done the hard work to set your website copy up for success.

Now, the question is how to take all that hard work and use it on your website. Here's where I have good news and bad news.

Let's start with the good news. You've identified the most important messages to your customers, cataloged and prioritized them, and done it in a repeatable way. As your business grows and changes or you find you're attracting new audiences, you have a process to rely on going forward.

It's time for the bad news. There's no one way to structure a website that guarantees success. Every business is different. Every audience and set of visitors to a website varies. What converts well on one site—whether it be a piece of copy, a type of layout, or graphics—won't necessarily create wins on another.

That doesn't mean you're up a proverbial creek with no paddle. I'm not about to leave you stranded after you've gotten this far. Instead, I'm going to show you how to approach some of the most important copy on your website based on the information and findings you've summarized; but before we dive into piecing together your copy, let's quickly chat about you and the goals your business needs to achieve.

Your website goals

Way back in the introduction, I talked about how your goals and those of your customers are inextricably tied. To achieve your goals, you need your customers to reach theirs. While we've spent the first two-thirds of the book talking all about your customers' needs, it's about time we address yours.

Each page of your website has a purpose. That purpose can range from educating visitors about who you are on an About page to providing them with a payment form on a Checkout page. Whatever that purpose is, it's connected to the higher goals you have for your website and, consequently, your business.

Unless your business is a hobby, your aim is to make a profit. One of your business goals may be to increase revenue by a certain percentage over the next year. If you're a web designer or consultant, your website will need to convert prospects into leads. That means you'll want to do things like directing visitors to your opt-in, giving them reasons to make it worthwhile to join your email list, and telling them what they can expect from working with you. If you have an e-commerce website, giving visitors a clear, frictionless path to purchasing your products will be essential.

Without a clear idea of what you need your website to do for your business, merely repeating your customers' messages back to them isn't enough. You may be helping them learn everything they want to know about what you're an expert in, but if you're not leading them down a path to hiring your services or buying your products, your business will end up with the short end of the stick.

Whether you're optimizing an existing website or starting from scratch, ask yourself the following question.

What job does my website have to get done?

We've used Jobs To Be Done Theory to assess how your customers approach your products and solutions. It's time to turn those ideas on your own business as it relates to your website.

Think of your website as one of your employees. What job is it supposed to be doing for you? If you have an existing website, would you fire it or sing its praises? Like your customers, you're hiring products and solutions, including your website. Consider the main struggle you're looking to overcome with the help of this digital employee. You may need higher quality leads hitting your inbox or your widgets sold without getting on the phone with a customer. Whatever that need is, your website better fulfill it. How your website gets its job done relies heavily on aligning your goals with those of your customers.

Aligning your goals and your customers' goals

When I helped a colleague optimize the home page for an online teaching platform to learn to code, a significant number of survey respondents told us they had a difficult time understanding how much value the programming courses provided. The main call to action on the home page directed visitors straight to the plans and pricing page, asking them to invest in a lot of video training before giving them the information they needed to make a decision.

Based on the voice of customer research, we decided to test out the following changes:

- A rewritten headline and sub-headline to highlight the specificity and unique quality of the courses, adding in phrases used over and over again by customers (including "easy to understand" and "step-by-step" along with the most sought after coding languages visitors wanted to learn)
- Copy below the fold that framed visitors' anxieties in the form of solutions the courses could provide (e.g. Choose X when other training programs move too fast)
- Button copy in the main call to action making it clear visitors would be led to a destination where they could learn more about how the courses worked ("Show Me How the Curriculum Works")
- A video featuring the owner and course instructor talking about what potential students could hope to gain by enrolling and addressing their most significant concerns

After making these changes, more people clicked the main call to action by over 66 percent. Plus, we saw a bump in sign-ups. The results indicated that visitors wanted more information before becoming paying customers. Asking those people to invest in the training too soon didn't help them achieve their goals on the site. Getting them on the right path made their decision process easier, and the conversions jump. It was a win-win for the customer and the business.

~

ONCE YOU FIND the intersection between your goals and those of your website visitors, you'll be ready to combine them with the rest of your voice of customer research to write conversion-friendly copy.

8

NAILING DOWN YOUR VALUE PROPOSITION

Not sure what a value proposition is? In simple terms, it's a statement that clearly articulates why your ideal customer should think twice about your product or solution. It conveys what sets your business apart from the pack and keys your prospects into what kind of value you can provide for them. Plus, it lets your website visitors know they have landed in the right place and will find what they need and what they want.

Whenever someone comes to your website, that person immediately needs to understand where they've landed and what's in it for them.

If you think back to Chapter 1, you'll remember the issue of limited attention spans. More than likely, your visitor has multiple tabs open in their browser. If they're anything like me, their brain is full of a myriad of random thoughts, like "*I better double-check and see if tomorrow is recycling day,"* "*Oh crap, we've run out of dog food!"* and "*What's the new black, and do I have any of it in my wardrobe?"*

This level of distraction is what you're competing against—people looking for answers to their questions or solutions to their problems while multi-tasking. They have only so much patience and mental bandwidth to figure out if you're selling anything they'll consider buying.

Value proposition does not equal mission statement

When I started working with a local nonprofit on a messaging strategy, I realized I needed to discuss value propositions early on. Not overthinking it, I threw out the term during one of our meetings. I found myself faced with blank stares.

After a few moments of silence, one of the women in the room said, "Oh, you mean a mission statement? Because we've got one of those." She went on to pull out a sheet of paper with a paragraph discussing all the things the company did.

I could understand her confusion. I had been talking about how it was essential to making it evident from the copy and design where their website visitors had landed.

Their mission statement had plenty of what and why in it.

The only problem was that they framed it from *their* perspective. That's what mission statements do. They focus on the aims and values of the business. Instead, a value proposition speaks directly to the customer's problem and how your product or solution will help fix it. That's what makes it fundamental to your marketing. Your value proposition is your outward-facing statement to the world.

If you're confused, think of it this way: Your customers want to know what's in it for them. They don't care about dull platitudes or rambling messages describing how great you think your business is. What they care about when they go to your website is getting what they need in the least amount of time possible.

~

What makes up a value proposition?

For most website pages, the value proposition consists of the main headline and sub-headline, along with benefit-driven bullet points at the top of the page.

Let's use a headline and sub-headline example from the homepage of Unbounce, a landing page builder application.

Build, Publish & A/B Test Landing Pages Without I.T.

The Mobile Responsive Landing Page Builder for Marketers

The headline lets you know what the solution does and what makes it different (no mad tech skills required). Their sub-headline tells you who should be using their solution (marketers who need mobile-responsive landing pages). Even their button copy ("Build a High-Converting Landing Page Now") informs you of the value you'll be getting.

In the few seconds it took you to read Unbounce's value proposition, you've been able to assess

- where you landed
- what type of business or solution is on offer
- what makes it special, different, or unique
- if the company or solution solves a problem you have
- if there's something in it for you, so you keep reading farther down the page

When you can put together all these things in a nifty little package as Unbounce has, your ideal customers will be far more likely to think there's a good reason to stay on your site.

Using your voice of customer research to write a value proposition

To write your value proposition, start by looking through your priority messages list and your customer mindset analysis to answer the following questions:

- What is my target audience's most significant pain point?
- How does my business, product, or solution solve that pain point?
- Why are the people in my target audience motivated to solve this problem? Or, what are they hoping to achieve?

Let's use our women's health coaching business as an example. We can see that in the Priority Messages list, the biggest problem (pain point) for these women is not finding a sustainable program.

Message Bucket	Prioritized Messages *(Most Referenced to Least)*
Struggle *What's the struggle to be resolved or the pain overcome with the help of your solution?*	• **Not able to find a sustainable program** • Tired of one-size-fits-all programs • No program fits my lifestyle • Too much conflicting information
The Fix *What's the job your solution needs to get done?*	• Takes the guesswork out of nutrition/exercise • Focuses on fitness and healthy eating, not just losing weight • Provides built-in accountability from a community of like-minded women
Hesitations *What makes your ideal customers worry about taking action?*	• Afraid this will be another program that fails • Ability to sustain motivation • Getting enough support and accountability • Is there a money-back guarantee?
State of awareness *How aware are your ideal customers of their problem or your solution?*	Product aware - prospects are aware of your brand, has tried other solutions but doesn't know why your brand is better than the rest
Differentiators *What's enticing about your solution that makes it the right fit for your customer?*	• Fully customized programs based on each woman's needs • Woman-only focused • One-on-one support from a certified coach
Success *How is life better after using your solution? What does success look like?*	• Increased confidence in body image • Improved health with balanced nutrition and exercise • Feels stronger and fitter

The coaching programs solve this problem by being customized to each person and having a built-in support network. This information comes straight from the customer mindset analysis.

How does your business solve your customers' problems? ***(Struggle + Fix)***	There's a tremendous amount of overwhelming information for these women. They don't know who to trust or follow. They know losing weight, eating healthier, and looking after their own needs takes work; but without the reassurance that they can achieve results with a program tailored to them, they're reluctant to try another. Customers need access to health and fitness coaching with built-in accountability that fits their schedule. Focus the copy on: • Easy to access, online programs customized to each person • Simple to follow exercises and nutrition information • The accountability aspect of others in the program • Testimonials from other women who have seen great results

What's motivating these women to seek out coaching? By looking at the "Success" column of the priority messages list, we see that the most frequently cited reason is a desire to feel more confident.

With those questions answered, the next step is to determine what makes this business unique and what's most important to prospects. Let's say our health coach prides herself on how easy her programs are to follow and customize. Going back through the priority messages list and customer mindset analysis, we know that the women in her target audience dislike cookie-cutter programs that don't fit their lifestyle. That means our health coach has positioned herself well. Her key differentiators are in line with what her customers want:

- Biggest pain point = Not able to stick with a program
- Solution to problem = Customized program with support
- Motivation/hoping to achieve = Feel more confident/comfortable in own body

Now we can develop a value proposition for the health coaching home page that speaks directly to the ideal customer.

Get the online coaching program to help you become your healthiest and fittest you

With one-on-one and group support, you can change your body and love yourself every step of the way

Along with the main headline and sub-headline, adding benefit-driven bullet points helps better qualify the value proposition. For instance, nowhere in the copy so far have I mentioned the fact that these programs are for women. That's an important fact that anyone landing on the page should understand quickly. An easy way to rectify the situation is to create another sub-headline and use it to introduce bullet points, like this:

Programs designed for women who want to:

- Stay motivated to reach their personal health goals
- Gain confidence while losing weight
- Stop being their own worst enemy when it comes to diet and exercise

If there's a subset of women whom our coach plans to target, clearly spelling that out is a bonus. Is the coaching specifically designed to help women over forty? New moms? Suddenly, "Programs designed for women..." becomes "Programs designed for women over forty..." Whatever qualification these women most identify with is the one to use.

A case for using a customer's words

Once you've sorted out the critical pieces of your value proposition, look through your pulled customer quotes and frequently used words to see where it makes sense to incorporate any of them into your headline, sub-headline, or bullet points.

For instance, I used the phrase "pasta that sells itself" in the headline for a fundraising home page.

Choose an easy-to-run fundraiser with pasta that sells itself

With Fun Pasta Fundraising, put the fun back in your fundraiser...and raise more money while you're doing it!

After going through all the testimonials and survey responses in my research, I found this particular phrase repeated over and over again. Parents and organizers of fundraisers seemed almost relieved that they finally had found a product to sell that people genuinely wanted to buy.

If you've ever been greeted at your front door by a well-meaning child selling less-than- edible-looking foodstuffs to raise money for an organization or activity, you can only imagine the appeal of coming face-to-face with high-quality pasta. It's a whole lot easier to convince yourself not only to buy but also to buy more.

While I filed this phrase under Success, it serves a dual purpose. Organizers of these fundraisers want a product that's easy to sell because they have concerns about raising enough money for their activity. How do I know? The research told me. So, making it clear they can run a fundraiser with "pasta that sells itself" helps alleviate those concerns. Once hooked, they can find the proof as they move farther down the page and into the website.

Uncover your value proposition

Based on your research and analysis, come up with a value proposition for your home page. To do that, you'll need to do the following:

- Determine your customers' biggest pain point, how your solution solves their problem, and how it will make their lives better.
- Pull out any customer quotes or frequently used words worth testing in your copy.
- Include your key differentiator, or what makes you unique.

Think beyond your headline when developing your value proposition. It can extend to your sub-headline, supporting bullet points, and any supporting copy your visitors first see upon landing on the page.

9

TYING TOGETHER YOUR FEATURES AND BENEFITS

When people go to write copy, nothing seems to confuse them more than the difference between features and benefits. You have a website you need to fill with copy, and your first inclination is to talk about all the components that make up your product or service. After all, isn't that why visitors are coming to your site? They need information so they can figure out if what you're selling is something they want.

You're not wrong. Customers need your offer details; otherwise, all they're reading about are their pains. Problems without solutions aren't going to help them. They're looking for answers. The challenge for you becomes balancing your customers' need for information and your genuine need to convey the value of what you're selling.

The key to this balancing act lies in telling your customers about the features of your product or service within the context of how they'll benefit from them. For instance, just listing the ingredients in your organic dog shampoo doesn't tell customers how their and their pooch's lives will be exponentially better after using it. You have to spell it out for them to tie in with what they care about most.

Before you can do that, you need to get comfortable identifying the difference between your features and the benefits that go along with them.

What are "features?"

Features are the items that make up your product or service. I like to think of them as the facts behind your offer. For an organic dog shampoo, this would be a feature:

Made with organic tea tree oil

That statement tells us about the "what" of the product. It's all fact without the "why."

While knowing what you're getting from your purchase is essential, rarely do features sell on their own. It's the benefits that do the heavy lifting in your copy.

What are "benefits?"

Benefits are the why behind your features. They give your customers an emotional, intangible reason to buy into your product or service. In a nutshell, benefits help answer that critical question people ask when they move through your site: *Why should I care?*

Here's an example of a benefit of using the organic dog shampoo:

Keep your dog safe from fleas and ticks without worrying about nasty chemicals.

Worry about diseases and fear of exposing myself and my pet to scary pesticides taps into two upsetting emotions. Telling me this product can make that worry and anxiety go away is compelling. It's a lot more convincing than being shown there's tea tree oil in the shampoo. Knowing I can keep my dog safe makes my life better—a huge selling point.

Determining key benefits

Do you remember way back in Chapter 1 when I talked about motivations and finding your customers' why? Figuring out the deep down, why behind your customers' motivation for seeking out what you're selling is a similar process to discovering the key benefits of your product or service. You start by asking why, and then you continue asking until you've gotten to the root of the emotional core.

Let's take the tea tree oil feature of the dog shampoo as our starting point.

Why is tea tree oil a vital ingredient in the shampoo?

Because it helps repel fleas and ticks naturally.

Why do I care if it repels fleas and ticks naturally?

Because I'd prefer that my dog doesn't get sick from the bugs or chemicals.

Why do I want my dog to be bug and chemical-free?

Because I love my dog and I don't want to be worried about him keeling over from a disease or bathing in pesticides.

Now that's the ticket! Immediately I understand how my world can be a better place with this tea tree-filled organic dog shampoo. That's the key benefit, and if you haven't noticed yet, it corresponds to the customer's deeper motivations.

Think of it this way; your key benefits should be the answer to what's keeping your customers up at night. It's the part of your copy that matches your customer's desire with the value your product or service can provide. Which brings me to a distinction between benefits that directly tie to a particular feature and those that you can attribute to your business as a whole. Those overarching benefits that go beyond features can speak to what makes you different.

Consider the online retailer Zappos. Their passion for customer service seeps into all of their messaging. How they approach keeping their customers happy is core to their company's ethos. You better believe that ethos counts as a big old benefit. And Zappos doesn't let you forget it. From their tagline, "Powered by service," to their Shipping and Returns page, it's everywhere.

How to apply your voice of customer research to your features and benefits

Now that you know the distinction between features and benefits, it's time to see how all that juicy voice of customer research can be used to your advantage when talking about them. The place to start is with a list of the features that make up your product, service, or solution. Once you've laid them out on the page, look at each closely, and determine if there's a compelling benefit you can attach to them.

You may find that you can assign several benefits to one feature, and you have to rack your brain to come up with even one for another feature. That's okay. It's worth the time to go through this process so you can compare what you think is important to your customers with what your research tells you is important.

Using our health coach example, a list of features for her coaching services packages might look like this:

- One-on-one coaching sessions via conference call
- Recordings of all the coaching sessions
- Customized diet and exercise plans
- Access to a private online community for coaching members
- E-mail support to answer questions

These are the items that make up her offerings, the things her customers will get when they pay. These features don't tell the visitors coming to her site why they matter. That's the job of the benefits.

Let's take a look at the "Customized diet and exercise plans" feature and map out the benefits associated with it so you can see how one looks.

Key benefits of a customized diet and exercise plan:

- No more obsessing about what to eat and how to exercise, because it's all spelled out
- Feel confident in your choices when you've got a plan geared toward setting you up for success

Both benefits speak to how this component of the packages will make customers' lives better. They tap into the motivations behind why someone looking for this type of service would choose it.

Comparing what you think is important with what your customers care about

Let's use our coaching program example to see how you can take your research and apply it to your features and benefits list. Go back through your priority messages list and pay particular attention to The Fix (aka job to be done) and Success buckets. These are the places where you'll find what kinds of features and benefits your customers care about most.

For instance, when we look at the list of what customers need this program to do for them, we find that taking the guesswork out of knowing what to eat and how to exercise tops the list.

The Fix

- Takes the guesswork out of nutrition/exercise
- Focuses on fitness and healthy eating, not just losing weight
- Provides built-in accountability from a community of like-minded women

Let's compare that with the features I came up with earlier in this chapter. The customized diet and exercise plan feature matches up with this top need. That means

I'd want to highlight this feature first by talking up its associated benefits.

Success

- Increased confidence in body image
- Improved health with balanced nutrition and exercise
- Feels stronger and fitter

Notice from the list above that increasing confidence is the number one desired outcome. I'd want to see how my most sought after feature might tap into that desire. Going back to the key benefits I came up with for the customized diet and exercise plan; the second one fits the bill:

Feel confident in your choices when you've got a program geared toward setting you up for success

Highlighting this benefit on the home or services page makes sense, given the hierarchy of messages we previously determined.

What does this whole feature/benefit thing look like on the page?

Let's take a real-life example from a brand that has become synonymous with the value of a product's features within its benefits: Apple.

Apple's copywriters have mastered the art of selling the experience of owning one of their products, not just the products themselves. When you read any of the copy on their product pages, the deeper emotional reasons why buying an iPhone, iPad, or computer will make your life better immediately draw you in.

> **Why there's nothing quite like iPhone**
>
> Every iPhone we've made – and we mean every single one – was built on the same belief. That a phone should be more than a collection of features. That, above all, a phone should be absolutely simple, beautiful, and magical to use.

In the above case, they tell you why the iPhone is greater than the sum of its parts (or features). Using an iPhone will be a "magical" experience. As you scroll down the page, you find out how. Each feature becomes a launchpad for something new and exciting you can do or create. Take the camera, with all of its enhanced features in the iPhone 6S. It has things like "Focus Pixels," "auto stabilization," and an "image signal processor." Sounds pretty cool, right? If you're a gadget geek, maybe. The copywriters at Apple understand that while those fancy-sounding features may pique your interest, they don't mean a lot on their own. They don't convey how they will make your everyday life better, more exciting, or entertaining. They use images to show you how amazing the photos you can take with your camera are; then, they tell you what those features can do for you.

> What does that all mean? It means we've taken care of the technology. All you have to do is find something beautiful and tap the shutter button for the best, most awe-inspiring photos you've ever taken.

The power in the copy comes from transforming lifeless features into conduits for capturing a moment in time that's relatable. Those "Focus Pixels" and "auto stabilization" features suddenly seem way more valuable when seen within the context of taking point-and-shoot photos of real-life things.

10

CLOSING THOUGHTS

If you've made it through the entire book, pat yourself on the back. You are light- years ahead of most business owners when it comes to thinking about communicating with the customer online.

Even if you only dip your toe into conducting customer research voice without diving headfirst, you've made an important step. You've shifted your mind-set away from making your website all about you and focusing on how to help your customers be successful.

Once you start talking to your customers, you'll get hooked

Doing all of this voice of customer research may seem tedious. I'd be lying if I said it's all rainbow sprinkles and unicorns. It takes time, energy, and a whole lot of brainpower. For most of us trying to keep our heads above water while running a business, these are three things that are usually in short supply.

But you might find something magical happens once you do start getting on the phone or exchanging emails with your clients. You learn things about your business and your offerings; you would never have found out otherwise. You gain insights into not only what's working and what's not working but also why your customers love what you do. Armed with that kind of knowledge, you'll wonder how you ever lived without it before.

RESOURCES AND NOTES

You can find additional information about voice of customer research along with articles I've written on my website at www.makementionmedia.com.

To get the worksheet template documents, go to www.makementionmedia.com/resources.

If you're interested in learning more about the references and examples cited in this book, find them here by chapter.

Introduction

- The statistics about customer research come from the Profitwell blog. Patrick Campbell, "Customer Research: Benchmarks and

Common Mistakes" Profitwell, Updated June 8, 2020, https://www.profitwell.com/blog/customer-research-benchmarks

- The statistics about customer satisfaction come from a Salesforce annual report. Conor Donegan, "State of the Connected Customer Report Outlines Changing Standards for Customer Engagement" June 12, 2019, https://www.salesforce.com/company/news-press/stories/2019/06/061219-g/

Chapter 1

The Norman Nielsen Group is one of the leaders in conducting and teaching UX research. Check out the following articles from NNG referenced in this chapter and the wealth of information on the rest of its website.

- Jakob Nielson, "How Long Do Users Stay on Web Pages?" September 12, 2011, https://www.nngroup.com/articles/how-long-do-users-stay-on-web-pages/

- Jakob Nielson, "How Users Read on the Web," October 1, 1997, https://www.nngroup.com/articles/how-users-read-on-the-web

- Kathryn Whitenton, "Satisficing: Quickly Meet

Users' Main Needs," March 30, 2014, https://www.nngroup.com/articles/satisficing/

- Adele Revella, one of the pioneers in persona work, talks about the need for verbatim quotes from customers that describe how they make purchase decisions in her 2015 book, *Buyer Personas: How to Gain Insight into Your Customer's Expectations, Align Your Marketing Strategies, and Win More Business.*

- The example about childcare through the lens of Jobs to Be Done Theory comes from the 2016 book, *Competing Against Luck: the Story of Innovation and Customer Choice* by Christensen, C. M., Hall, T., Dillon, K., & Duncan, D. S.

- The story about Intercom along with any quotes referenced can be found in a Harvard Business Review article by Christensen, C. M., Hall, T., Dillon, K., & Duncan, D. S. (January 24, 2020). "Know Your Customers' 'Jobs to Be Done'" https://hbr.org/2016/09/know-your-customers-jobs-to-be-done

Chapter 2

- The headline and sub-headline used as an

example is taken from the Spotify homepage from May 2020. https://www.spotify.com/us/

- The subscriber numbers for Spotify are taken from an online article in Variety by Todd Spangler (February 5, 2020). Spotify Zooms to 124 Million Premium Subscribers in Q4, Record Quarterly Gain Driven by Promos. https://variety.com/2020/digital/news/spotify-q4-2019-premium-subscribers-podcast-investments-1203493393/

- I reference April Dunford's thoughts on market categories from her 2019 book, *Obviously Awesome: How to Nail Product Positioning so Customers Get It, Buy It, Love It.* She provides a step-by-step guide to positioning and some helpful insights that can be applied to messaging.

- You can read more about the Ambiguity Effect in the following source: Deborah Frisch and Jonathan Baron, "Ambiguity and Rationality," Journal of Behavioral Decision Making 1, no. 3 (1988).

- The ideas about a customer's state of awareness and existing desires come from Eugene

Schwartz's 1966 book, *Breakthrough Advertising.* This is a must read for any copywriter.

Chapter 3

- Steve Krug's 2014 book, *Don't Make Me Think, Revisited: A Common Sense Approach to Web Usability* is the source referenced in this chapter. You will find practical takeaways from this book you can apply to any website project.

- Noah Kagan's story is from "How One Survey Created Insane Results," OkDork , October 14, 2013, https://okdork.com/2013/10/14/how-to-use-surveys-to-get-insane-results/ .

- You can learn more about The foot-in-the-door technique in the following journal article: Jonathan L. Freedman and Scott C. Fraser, "Compliance without Pressure: The Foot-in-the-Door Technique," Journal of Personality and Social Psychology 4, no. 2 (1966): 195–202.

- The pop-up survey numbers come from Michael Nadelman on the Qualaroo blog, "What Is Typically Considered a Good Response Rate?" Updated January 2020, http://help.qualaroo.

com/hc/en-us/articles/201484047-What-is-typically-considered-a-good-response-rate

- The idea of commitment and consistency comes from Robert B. Cialdini's 1993 book, *Influence: The Psychology of Persuasion. (rev. ed.).*

Chapter 8

- The headline and sub-headline copy used as an example from Unbounce is taken from their homepage website in 2016. While this copy no longer exists on their current website, it continues to serve as a helpful value proposition example.

Chapter 9

- The copy used as examples from the Apple website is taken from the launch of their iPhone 6s in 2016. While this copy no longer exists on their current website, it continues to serve as a helpful example of how to tie features to benefits.

ABOUT THE AUTHOR

Jennifer Havice is a messaging consultant and customer researcher who helps subscription model businesses determine who their best-fit customers are, what makes them tick, and how to craft compelling copy to turn more prospects into raving fans.

Jen has consulted for both B2B and B2C growing subscription businesses. Her book, Finding the Right Message, continues to be the go-to resource for both copywriters and marketers interested in learning how to conduct voice of customer research to improve their messaging.

You can find her chasing after two quirky wire-haired pointers and three large horses when she's not sifting through survey responses or clarifying value propositions. She lives and works in the Twin Cities – or as she affectionately likes to call it, the land of 10,000 hot dishes.

Connect online:

Twitter: @jenhavice

LinkedIn: @jenhavice

Website: www.makementionmedia.com

Printed in Great Britain
by Amazon

52488379R00095